TIMOTHY STARR

church planting

always in season

TIMOTHY STARR

church planting

always in season

INDEX

FOREWARD

I consider it an honour to be asked to write the *Forward* to this challenging book by A. T. Starr. In 1971, as a member of the Executive Council of the Fellowship of Evangelical Baptist Churches, I participated in the appointment of Mr. Starr as our Fellowship Field Representative. Since that favourable introduction, I have been in a position to see him in action and, ever since 1974, when he became Home Mission Secretary, I have received from him monthly reports of his work, for publication in the *Evangelical Baptist.*

While others may have been aware of the course of study which he was pursuing under the direction of members of the faculty of *Luther Rice Seminary,* I knew nothing about those studies but I watched with delight and amazement the growth of our Home Mission thrust under his guidance. To me this book is not the fulfillment of an academic assignment, it is the record of how the Church Planting Miracle of the 70's was carried out in Canada under the direction of A.T. Starr and his associates on the Home Mission Board of the Fellowship. I predict that this book will become a manual for Church Planters, not only in the Fellowship, but among Evangelical Baptists in all parts of the English-speaking world.

I have long been attracted to the traditional Southern Baptist concept of the church. To be sure, that position may have been overstated by some, but I am convinced that the preaching which regards the assembly of God's people as the church which Jesus said He would build, is one of the best answers to the ecumenism of our day. Timothy Starr does not even state his position with respect to the doctrine of the church; he seems to be saying, "Men, let's not waste time talking, just get busy and plant churches!"

How he found the time to pursue his studies, of which the writing of this book was only a part and, at the same time, to give leadership in the building of dozens of churches all across Canada, must ever be a source of amazement. As now he undertakes even greater tasks, I join with his many friends and say, "God bless you, Dr. Timothy Starr, may you bow abide in strength".

Dr. J. R. Armstrong.

LET ME SAY SOMETHING BEFORE I BEGIN TO WRITE

"No man is an island" writes John Doone and this is true. Two men have influenced my life in home mission work: William Turnwall and Jack Watt.

William Turnwall served as the Secretary of Home Missions of the Baptist General Conference from 1945 until July, 1962. During his tenure of leadership he introduced innovations that have served to multiply home mission churches in the United States and Canada. Under his leadership the following functions were commenced: the Revolving Building Trust, Church Extension Fund, Opportunity, Benevolent Fund, God's Invasion Army, and mission work in Alaska, Mexico, Virgin Islands and among American Indians in Minnesota.

His first visit with me was in Cedar Rapids, Iowa. Serving as a student pastor and founding a church, I was looking for guidance and reinforcement. Bill Turnwall had a listening ear and an understanding heart. This was typical of the man who lived out of a suitcase, travelling from coast to coast by train, car, bus and plane. With his usual zeal he seized the opportunity in Cedar Rapids and provided me with a friendship that lasted through the years. I owe much to him for his ministry and for the privilege of travelling with him to many states.

The Turnwalls provided me with warm hospitality on numerous occasions. I recall family devotions in their home. They were fine parents seeking always to honour the Lord. It is not surprising that their three children are active in the Lord's work.

Jack Watt, general Secretary of the Fellowship of Evangelical Baptist Churches in Canada from July, 1965 through October, 1977, was the man God used to open the home mission door in my home land. Jack Watt has been God's man for the Fellowship. In 1965 there were 303 churches. Upon his retirement there were 400 Fellowship Baptist Churches. Much of this growth is due to his vision and leadership.

It was Jack Watt who brought my name to the Executive Council to serve as the Fellowship Field Representative in 1971. This led to the position of the first Fellowship Home Mission Secretary in 1974. In this office Jack Watt has given me much spiritual and moral backing.

One of the greatest things one man can do for another is to trust him. Jack Watt entrusted me with leadership. He was a master in delegating responsibility to others. Not being able to do all the work himself, and with rapid expansion of the Fellowship, he sought to assemble a team of men to assist as co-workers. His confidence and support have been greatly appreciated.

Jack Watt has led me to launch out into the deep again and again. He would remind me that our pastors will support home missions if they see that the job is being done. This type of vision and support has resulted in the planting of churches in fields hitherto unknown to the Fellowship.

To these two beloved servants of the Lord, I am profoundly grateful. They have shaped and prepared me for home mission work. The following pages serve as a tribute to their lives and ministries.

The outline gives twenty-one topics dealing with church planting. Each chapter provides information, in point form, and gives suggestions pertaining to the topic. This is followed by an actual case study of how that particular topic was developed. The emphasis is on the practical side of opening new churches.

The reader will readily discern that all the case studies are about church planters working with the Fellowship of Evangelical Baptist Churches in Canada. However, the material is applicable to pastors of most denominations engaged in church planting.

I have employed the simplest method of entering the source of information used. You will note that each bibliographical entry, though alphabetized, is numbered consecutively. The first number in a quotation directs you to the bibliography and the second number gives you the page from which the material comes.

A word of appreciation to Miss Carolyn Dyment, and Dr. John Armstrong who read the manuscript and offered many excellent suggestions, also to Belle Bulloch our proof-reader and Mary Finch my secretary.

Finally, a word of gratitude to God for Hazel my wife. Next to salvation, Hazel has been the greatest blessing to me. This woman of God, esteemed mother of our four children, is an excellent example of a church planter's wife.

A. Timothy Starr

Chapter 1

Campbell Baptist Church
Windsor, Ontario

ACCORDING TO THE RULE

A prominent evangelist came to Toronto, Canada. Within a few years he had built up a congregation of about 1700 people. Resigning his pastorate to return to school, he remarked to a fellow pastor: "I am fearful that I am leaving behind a crowd but not a church." There is a difference!

It is not hard to draw a crowd. Many have tried it with success. You may feed them doughnuts. You may treat them to fried chicken. You may even have the world's largest banana split. Do this week after week and you will soon have a crowd. But what happens when the feeding stops?

There is truth to the expression that how a movement starts it will probably end. Although this does not apply to every church it certainly should be given serious consideration. Jesus Christ mentioned about building on a rock in Matthew 7:25. Too many build upon the quick sands of expediency. A church needs the right foundation if it is going to stand the test of time.

The first thing in building a church is to understand what it is. This leads us to seek out the definition of a church. What is the first thought that comes to your mind when you hear the word church? Pews? Organ? Pulpit? Those who respond with a similar answer are thinking in terms of a visible building. Actually the word church in the Greek is ECCLESIA. It is found 115 times in the New Testament. The vast majority of the references are to a local assembly of believers in Jesus Christ. Buildings and equipment are secondary. They do not have any bearing on the meaning of a church.

Many definitions have been given for a church. One of the best is that of Dr. Elmer Towns: "A church is an assembly of baptized believers, in whom Christ dwells, under the discipline of the Word of God, organized for evangelism, education, fellowship and worship; administering the ordinances and reflecting the spiritual gifts (73:157)." This definition covers four important truths in the perspective of a church. Follow these and you will build "According to the rule".

DEF OF THE CHURCH

I. The Authority of the Word of God

This is primary in the New Testament. The church is seen as a type in the Old Testament. Our Lord promised He would build His church (Matt. 16:18). The actual birth of the church took place on the Day of Pentecost (Acts 2:41-47). The Epistles furnish the doctrine and order for churches (I Tim. 3:14,15). The Book of Revelation reveals the culmination.

The implications of building a church according to the New Testament are far reaching. It means that you look to the New Testament for guidance as to the organization and procedure. It means that those who unite with such a church are recognizing the moral and ethical teaching of the New Testament and are willing to subject themselves to the discipline of a local church (Gal. 6:1).

Following the New Testament teaching saves the church members many problems. Take for an example the qualifications for a pastor. Can a pastor be a divorced man? Several denominations have debated this in the past five years. The New Testament speaks of the pastor and marriage and answers this question in I Tim. 3:1-7.

INTERPRETIVE SITUATION!

II. The Assembly of Believers

Many churches have a mixed membership of both saved and unsaved people. This comes about through carelessness or through rushing people into membership. The description of the Karen Church in Burma is a fine example of how one church went about the manner of receiving members:

Does anyone get the idea that church membership was easy to come by in these early days? We need only to pay attention to the requirements made. Each candidate was

> *expected to give evidence of a new life in Christ that would satisfy the Karen Church itself. In its decision its vote had to be unanimous. Once his language was reduced to writing the candidate had to know how to read. He had to abstain from liquor, a common weakness of the Karens and had to promise to follow the morality revealed in the Bible. Exclusion from the church for such as did not keep the faith was not a rare occurence.*
>
> *The above shows the type of requirements followed by the Karen Church of Burma in the early days under the ministry of Adoniram Judson and George Boardman (13:77,78).*

You may recognize that some of the requirements are not New Testament, such as the ability to read. However, there is a sense in which the Karen Church sought to maintain a membership of believers. It is interesting to note that this church experienced excellent growth. After all that is said and done, it is His church, and God's work done in God's way is going to have the favour of God.

III. The Administration of the Ordinances

To multitudes of church people there is a mysterious aspect of salvation attached to baptism and the Lord's Supper. Actually, these were given to believers and have no saving merit. It is better to refer to them as "ordinances in place of the commonly used word "sacrament". Dr. Gordon J. Johnson has rightly said:

> *Many churches use the term 'sacrament' in place of ordinance. We as Baptists do not. We use the term 'ordinance' because these are actually outward rites symbolizing inner spiritual experiences 'ordained' by the Lord Himself. The words 'sacrament', as it is used by other groups, indicates that God does something to the individual who participates no matter what his spiritual condition may be. We as Baptists believe the ordinances bring blessing in response to faith and obedience to the Lord's command (45:39).*

Baptism is the initial ordinance for believers. It naturally follows conversion. It is an outward sign of that which has taken place within the heart. It might be likened to photography. Snap your picture, the image is transferred to the film. This is conversion. When the picture is developed you see what has taken place. This is baptism.

Although there are three methods commonly used to baptize today: pouring, sprinkling and immersion, only the latter portrays Romans 6:1-6. Historian Kohannes talks about the early meaning of baptism and quotes Professor A. Deissmann:

> *The earliest generations of Christians were easily able to understand the mystical significance of the separate stages of baptism as becoming dead, buried, and risen with Christ, because having been baptized as adults they had an indestructible living recollection of their baptism performed by immersion (78:27).*

The word baptize is in Greek, BAPTIZO, which means to dip, immerse, submerge or overwhelm. Baptizing believers by immersion is following the New Testament pattern and as such is the only method acceptable.

The question has been often asked if there should be a waiting period before a believer is baptized. Edwin Anderson gives a fine answer.

> *Baptism is the first command of Christ to the new-born believer. No other obligation stands between conversion and baptism. That is why converts in the New Testament were baptized immediately after they accepted Christ, and before they partook of the Lord's Supper. As good soldiers of the Lord, they did not hesitate to put on His uniform. Faithful pastors and evangelists ought to keep their congregation always informed as to the prerequisites, meanings, and obligations of baptism so that their converts will be prepared at the time of conversion for the ordinance. Then lengthy waiting periods of instruction will not be needed (2:56).*

Should a person be rebaptized? Yes, if the individual was not immersed as a believer. One of my classmates at the Northern Baptist Theological Seminary, Chicago, Freeman Schmidt, accepted a call to his first church. He was planning his first baptismal service. He thought back to his own experience of baptism. He recalled how as a boy he responded to an invitation along with several others in his Sunday School class. He remembered how several years later he realized that he had not been born again. During a series of special meetings he came to a realization of his need and confessed Jesus Christ as His Saviour. It occured to him that he was going to baptize believers although he himself had not been immersed as a believer. The following Sunday, before baptizing others, he himself after giving a word of testimony, was baptized by a guest pastor. You can imagine the spiritual impact of the service.

Many pastors have been faced with the following problem. A fine Christian presents himself for membership. He explains that, after conversion, he was baptized by pouring or sprinkling. That is to say, he submitted to a form of baptism as a public confession of his faith in Jesus Christ. Before receiving him into membership, we would have the individual immersed. That is being consistent with the New Testament. We cannot accept any other form of baptism if the New Testament is going to be our guide.

Why do we not recognize pouring or sprinkling? There are several reasons. These modes of baptism are not biblical. They do not carry out the symbol of believer's baptism (Romans 6:3,4). They do not represent the way our Lord was baptized (Matthew 3:13-17). They do not represent the method used in the Book of Acts (Acts 8:38,39).

While baptism by immersion is the initial ordinance to be administered once for each believer, the Lord's Supper is the recurring ordinance. It is carried on by the local church. It is for believers who are walking in obedience to Jesus Christ and in Christian fellowship. This is why Paul calls for personal examination before the Lord's Supper (I Cor. 11:28). Thus it has nothing to do with bringing us salvation. It has much to do with our personal walk before God and fellow believers.

How often should a church observe the Lord's Supper? The New Testament does not lay down a set formula. However, it gives the spirit of the service (I Cor. 11:26). The question is not the number of times but the manner and spirit with which we partake of the elements.

The bread reminds us of His body given for us. The cup is a symbol of His blood, shed on the cross, for the remission of our sins. Jesus Christ has given wholly of Himself for our salvation. He held nothing back.

Andrew Murray in commenting on the passage: "Take eat; this is my body which is given for you (Luke 22:9)" says:

> *When the Lord says, this, He points out to us that His body is not so much His as it is ours, since He received it and suffered it to be broken on the cross, not for His own sake, but for ours; and that He now also desires that we should look upon it and appropriate it as our own possession. Thus, with His body, He gives Himself to us, and desires that we should take Him. The fellowship of the Lord's Supper is a fellowship of giving and taking. Blessed giving, blessed taking (54:61).*

Charles H. Spurgeon has given real significance to the table of our Lord with the verses of his hymn:

Amidst us our Beloved stands,
And bids us view His pierced hands;
Points to the wounded feet and side,
Blest emblems of the crucified.
What food luxurious loads the board,
When, at His table, sits the Lord!
The wine how rich, the bread how sweet,
When Jesus deigns the guests to meet!
If now, with eyes defiled and dim,
We see the signs, but see not Him;
O, now His love the scales displace,
And bid us see Him face to face!
Thou glorious Bridegroom of our hearts,
Thy present smile a heaven imparts!
O, lift the veil, if veil there be,
Let every saint Thy glory see.

IV. The Association of Believers

This aspect of a New Testament Church involves the whole field of interpersonal relationships and world evangelization.

The theme of the Epistle to the Philippians is fellowship in action. Paul describes two types of fellowship: negative and positive. Negative fellowship ought not to be a part of a local church. An illustration of a negative fellowship is given in Phil. 4:2. It would appear that Euodia and Syntyche were not in accord, though both were active in the church. "I beseech Euodia, and beseech Syntyche." They were so far apart that the Apostle Paul used a verb. Many times this type of negative relationship has hindered the work of a local church.

A positive type of fellowship is illustrated in Phil. 2:19. J.B. Phillips has given the following on this verse: "But I hope in the Lord Jesus that it will not be long before I can send Timothy to you...I have nobody else with a genuine interest in your well-being." What a commentary on the life of a fellow believer! Actually, this is what the local church is for; — believers reinforcing believers; each believer ministering to his brethren.

A church must likewise have a vision of the harvest field. Acts 1:8 gives the perspective for missions, at home and abroad. It has been well stated that "The light that shines farthest shines brightest nearest home." A church without a vision will soon have no mission. Dr. Medford Jones has phased it well:

There is a possibility that the classical great commissions have served, in a sense, to be self-defeating. Few people seem to get excited over 'going into all of the world'. This is because the grand commission is difficult to emotionalize and grasp by the individual 'work-a-day' member of the church. However, the great commission can become very real and very significant to any member of the church when it is translated into terms of local church growth and church multiplication. Paul's ministry illustrated this. Any one can understand how the growth of church "A" in locality "D" is actually accomplishing God's purpose... thus God purposed from the very beginning that local churches are to be His means of discipling the nations. Let us face the fact, that, if discipling is done, it will be done at the level of the local congregation. The church is God's primary strategic weapon. Every church from its beginning should be focused toward outreach and self-reproduction (100:4,5).

Now it is one thing to know the "rule" but another thing to follow it. Some pastors are timid to declare it from the beginning. Pastor George Bell of Oakwood Baptist Church, Toronto, Canada, in his church planting course at Central Baptist Seminary, tells his students:: "Some church planters, in the interests of short-term gains, try a non-denominational approach. The compromise required sets like cement and, when eventually a biblical position is taken, the work suffers a serious set-back."

An Example of a Church Planter With a Right Perspective

Dr. Jack H. Watt is a prime example of a church planter with the right perspective. He moved to the City of Windsor in 1944. The war clouds were still hanging over the world although the Allies were well on their way to a total victory. The City of Windsor was bursting at its seams geared up for the national war effort. Hundreds of new homes had been erected to house the war plant workers. The auto industry and related shops were dedicated to winning the war.

Three small churches had come together to form the Campbell Baptist Church. Total membership was forty. Almost half of these were children. It was a challenge. Knowing the perspective of a New Testament Church, Jack Watt set out to establish the same to the glory of God.

His first step was to organize the Sunday School. He put to work all who could possibly teach a class. The young people were organized with programs that challenged them to serve the Lord and live for Him.

He next set up a visitation program. At first it included just two, Jack and his wife. They started knocking on doors and following up prospects. Others saw their example and joined them in the task. Soon, men and women and youth from different social strata were visiting throughout the community.

A new building was soon needed. The 200 seats had been filled and extra chairs were used in the aisles. Enthusiasm was running high, but there was no money for a building.

Attending a board meeting in Toronto, Jack Watt was inspired by advice given to another brother: "You can do anything you want to do if God is leading you to do it". The task seemed small from that day onward. The people approved plans for a building. Property was purchased. Financing was prepared by arranging a first mortgage bond issue. The Lord performed miracles and the church got all that was needed.

Attendances in the new building rose. Soon the church had to begin thinking of extra space. The building now had 600 seats in the auditorium with extra rooms on the first and second floors besides a full basement. All possible areas were overflowing. A record attendance of 1,141 was registered in the Sunday School. The key to such growth was the Pastor's Adult Bible Class which regularly had between 350 and 400 in attendance.

The church recognized the necessity of getting more room or losing a lot of children as well as adults. A legion hall across the street was rented. Here the Junior Department met with 175 in attendance. Later a gas station next door to the church was secured for a parking lot. This was followed by the purchase of an eight family apartment building. This became a Christian Education building. Soon the church filled it too!

What are some of the results of such a growth? Some 700 to 800 were baptized during the ministry of Jack Watt at Campbell Baptist Church. Others were called into the ministry. Mrs. Linda Watson is serving in Japan under the Foreign Board of the Fellowship of Evangelical Baptist Churches in Canada. Rev. John Turanksy is an Instructor in Christian Education and Practical Ministries at the Western Conservative Baptist Seminary, Portland, Oregon. Miss Emily Turanksy is Dean of Women and Professor of Religious Education at Central Baptist Seminary, Toronto, Canada. Rev. Robert Baker is pastor of the Harriston Baptist Church, Harriston, Ontario. These and others are in active service.

This type of ministry results from the blessing of God upon a pastor who builds "According to the Rule". Jack Watt, responding to the question, What is a church? replied:

A New Testament church according to the Scriptures, is a body of believers who have been immersed (baptized) and who have voluntarily banded themselves together to worship the Lord, to observe the two New Testament ordinances of baptism and the Lord's Supper and to carry out, as the Holy Spirit enables them, the injunctions of the great commission.

Please note, they are believers. Through faith in Christ they have been made new creatures in Him. In their being baptized they have given witness to their position in Christ, dead to sin and alive unto God.

Note further, they have banded together. This, voluntarily and by agreement, and have made themselves a responsible body for the tasks outlined.

This led to a second question dealing with authority. To this Jack Watt said: "There is no authority recognized by the members of a Baptist Church except the Headship of Christ. He is the great Head of the Church. We recognize the Holy Spirit as the Administrator, for He guides each one and fills each one for the tasks assigned."

In dealing with a basic organization, he says: "Once a church has been brought into being by the voluntary banding together of some baptized believers, an organizational structure should be agreed upon for the initial period of the church's existence and ministry."

The two main officers of a local church are spelled out in I Tim. 3. The opening seven verses deal with the role of a pastor. It is helpful to note the description of a pastor and his role, according to Jack Watt, from his study of the Word

Scripturally the pastor is the undershepherd of the flock. He is responsible for caring for them in their spiritual lives. His task involves feeding the flock with the Word, that they may grow thereby. He should see to their training in spiritual things.

The pastor is a leader and should know the way God would have His people go and lead them in it. He should not abdicate this responsibility to any other.

The pastor is not a driver. The people should follow readily where he leads, if indeed it is apparent he is in the will of God. To attempt to drive them without going before is to ask for trouble.

The pastor should lead all business meetings of the church and see to it that all things are done decently and in order.

Taking up the role of deacons, Jack Watt suggests:

> *A deacon is planned by the great Head of the Church to be a*
> *help at all times to the pastor. His assistance to the pastor is*
> *invaluable if they work together in their God-given task.*
>
> *Deacons will help in visitation of the sick and needy. They*
> *can and should be soul winners who visit the homes of*
> *prospects for salvation and point those prospects to Jesus*
> *Christ. They should bring forward, at the invitation, any*
> *they have led to the Lord and introduce them to the pastor.*
> *The deacons of the church sitting as an advisory council to*
> *the pastor can make their service a source of strength and*
> *comfort to him.*

Churches differ as to the method used in welcoming new
members into their fellowship. Jack Watt suggests the following:

> *It is the accepted custom to have every prospective new*
> *member interviewed by a deacon or two or by all together.*
> *This is satisfactory in many cases but it is not necessarily the*
> *Scriptural method.*
>
> *The pastor should satisfy himself that the candidate for*
> *baptism and / or membership is truly born again before he*
> *baptizes that one or recommends him to the church for*
> *membership. This should be so, even though deacons or*
> *others have interviewed him. If the pastor has been in his*
> *task long enough to have gained the confidence of people*
> *they are often quite willing to accept his recommendation*
> *alone. A born again baptized believer who has moved into*
> *the area from a New Testament church may be received into*
> *membership by giving the pastor or deacons the story of*
> *his / her conversion and Christian experience. On this the*
> *individual may be recommended for membership.*
>
> *A baptized believer may ask the church to write for a letter*
> *of recommendation and dismissal from his former Baptist*
> *Church and thus be received.*

God is honouring pastors who are near to His heart and
precious in His sight. My first pastor, Dr. T. T. Shields, for many
years, pastor of the historic Jarvis Street Baptist Church,
Toronto, has given an excellent description of the church of God:

> *The church of God may be described as the Lord's*
> *masterpiece in which He delights to display His greatest*
> *skill. 'The heavens declare the glory of God; and the fir-*
> *mament showeth His handywork.' The whole universe is the*
> *work of His fingers. He has ordained the things that are.*
> *And yet of all the things that God has made that which is*

nearest to His heart, and upon which He has displayed His greatest skill, is His own church (95).

Chapter 2

OPPORTUNITY KNOCKING, ARE YOU THERE?

We are now founding colleges at the rate of twenty or more a year here in North America (42:152). By 1990 this will be increased to one a week! This suggests the magnitude of the growth and development expected in the Christian community. Evangelicals must take into consideration the challenge of an increased population. One well-known expert in church growth said recently that we need fifty-thousand new congregations in the United States and Canada tomorrow (6:43). *why?*

What should our attitude be in response to the growing needs of an expanding population, which knows little of God or the Bible? In I Cor. 2:3 you will note the attitude of Paul: "And I was with you in weakness, and in fear, and in much trembling." He was overwhelmed with the prospects of going to Corinth. He sensed the difficult road ahead. Here was a city, ruled by Rome, a centre of Greek commerce. As such it was one of the wealthiest cities of the first century. The Corinthians were a proud and wicked people. Corinth has been nicknamed the "Vanity Fair" of the Roman Empire. What a challenging centre for a church! Paul came with a certain sense of fear of the unknown and he recognized his weakness. We would do well to adopt his attitude.

"Opportunity is knocking" today. Let us consider several areas and note the example of a church planter who "was there" and responded to the call.

I. Consider the Potential in our Anticipated Increased Population

In the last fifteen years several of our North American cities have doubled in population. The two main cities of Alberta, Edmonton and Calgary, are examples of such a growth. Within ten years Calgary is expected to double again. In the year 2000 it is expected that the world population will be more than six billion people, double the population today (42:1). The population of the United States will be close to 340 million. The population of Canada will grow from 22,500,000 today to 35,000,000. Now consider the number of new churches needed to cope with such growth.

II. Consider the Potential in our Unchurched Population Today

The majority of people in Average Town, North America, do not attend a church of any denomination. In some centres the church attendance is at a very low ebb. One case study was done on Aurora, Ontario, where the population is just over 15,000. In many ways it is a typical Ontario community, if there is such a community. It is overwhelmingly white and Protestant. In a 1976 survey it was discovered that in the only two evangelical churches of the city, the Sunday morning attendance was under 100!

Rev. William Phillips, Secretary of the French Board of the Fellowship of Evangelical Baptist Churches in Canada, tells of scores of towns in the Province of Quebec, without a single evangelical church. And this is true of many areas in North America. Ralph Neighbour rightly says:

> *We begin to realize that one of the greatest untapped mission fields in the world remained in the United States! I am referring to the mission field of unchurched, pagan, couldn't care Americans who gave up religion a generation or more ago. They are to be found from the Atlantic to the Pacific and represent an evergrowing percentage of the American population. They literally live in the shadow of church buildings; yet churches are not even able to communicate successfully with them (56:21)!*

III. Consider the Potential in our Inner Cities

The urban centres have increased to the extent that we now use the term megalopolis. Imagine a single city in Ontario extending from Oshawa on the east to Kitchener on the west, to

Barrie on the north with Lake Ontario on the south. In the United States you have the centres of Chicago, Los Angeles and New York. Can one envision the multitudes of people without Christ, lost in the inner cities.

Ninety percent of the population of North America will soon be living in cities. Countless city dwellers are asking: "Who am I?" and "Who cares?" Where are the Evangelical churches to help? There is no question but that the city is one of the greatest frontiers facing the Evangelical church today. Giant apartment complexes, city decay and the shifting tides of people present the church with a challenging harvest field.

The sad reality is that in many areas the Evangelical church has retreated to the plush suburban communities. In 1976 a large Evangelical church sold a choice site just one kilometer from the University of Toronto. The congregation moved to a developing borough in the northern part of the city. The building was sold to the Hare Krishna. Where once the auditorium was filled with the praises of God now there are praises to an unknown God. Looking back over this event, one can see where Evangelicals should have made a more concerted effort to hold such a strategic site. Yet this is just one of many illustrations where the inner city has been deserted by Evangelicals.

Perhaps one of the problems is that Evangelicals have failed to keep up with the changes urbanization has made upon the lifestyle of people. Warren Rust said: "Urbanization has many characteristics... mobility of persons, changes in transportation systems and patterns, adjustments of massive proportions in housing patterns, communication media, educational systems, economic resources, etc. These changing forces are all segments of society. The backward look is not viable. Cities change people and people change churches (61:2)."

IV. Consider the Potential in our Ethnic Population

Most major cities in North America have large ethnic and cultural groupings. In Toronto, for one example, there are over 100,000 Asians, 60,000 West Indians, 400,000 Italians, 40,000 Portuguese, 33,000 Filipinos etc. Is the Evangelical church responsible for these people? For years we have sent our choicest youth to their native lands. Now God has honoured us by placing a mission field at the very front door of our churches.

Can these people be reached? The Home Mission Board of the Fellowship of Evangelical Baptist Churches in Canada invited V. P. Philips of South India to be a missionary to the Asians in

Toronto. As a result the Lord has used him to reach many Asians for Christ who are now active in a local church. A number of students have been reached in our universities who might well become leaders in the future. The same is true of Godfrey Catanus who was appointed to establish a Filipino Church. Within four months over 200 of his own people had been touched by the new church. Mario Bruno was appointed in January, 1978, to start a church for the Italian population in Toronto. The Home Mission Board of the Fellowship believes that it is easier to reach people from other cultures through a pastor born and raised in that particular background.

V. Consider the Potential in our Mobile Society

It is a well known fact that our population is transient. In some areas it is twenty percent, as among low cost housing and apartment dwellers. Many families move on the average of every five years. This presents a great opportunity to reach people. Moving to a new community can bring about new buying habits. People are open to suggestions where shopping may be done. As a result, organizations such as Welcome Wagon and Civic Newcomers Associations have been established to encourage new residents to visit the enterprises they represent. These business firms on the assumption that if they can please a new customer, they may continue to hold their business. To a certain degree the same principle works for the church.

One particular pastor along with his wife worked closely with newcomers. In three cities they organized a newcomer service for the express purpose of getting in touch with new residents and encouraging them to attend their services. These contacts produced a number of excellent members who later became leaders.

VI. Consider the Potential in the Multitudes of Church Members whose Spiritual Needs are not Being Met

Three serious problems face many of the North American churches today: apostasy, apathy and absenteeism.

Apostasy has such a deep root in some churches that pastors can now deny the virgin birth of Jesus Christ and the members do nothing about it. Liberal preachers have publicly set apart certain portions of the Bible as myth. Dr. Harold Lindsell refers to an article from Newsweek where a survey was taken of the beliefs of 521 clergy and laymen attending the National

Council of Churches General Assembly in Miami Beach in 1966. "Nearly two-thirds believe in God (this means that one third do not), and more than half — 58 percent — confidently regard Jesus as Divine.... Only one in four accepts Biblical miracles (43:145)." As a result many people in the pews are bewildered.

Apathy is a careless attitude towards the lost people of a community. This spirit of indifference spreads coldness through a congregation. It is demonstrated by a decreased interest in the spiritual ministry of a local church. Attendances at prayer meetings decline. Fewer come to teach in the Sunday School. There is a lack of interest in visitation work. "Let George do it" has become the unspoken motto.

VERY TRUE!

Absenteeism is a problem in many churches. Compare the Sunday morning attendance at your church with the number of members. In most Evangelical churches the attendance exceeds the membership. In most liberal churches the number on the membership roll exceeds the morning service attendance.

As a result, an untold number of church members are looking for a church that is real! This is our day of Evangelicals. Whereas Sunday School attendance is declining in liberal churches, it is growing in many Evangelical churches. Parents with growing families are looking for a church where their children may receive training for their lives. Middle aged people are looking for friends on whom they can count. Older people are searching for a faith as they face sickness and death. Yes, this is our day.

We have the potential to evangelize our continent through local churches. Melvin Hodges states: "The greatest contribution that a missionary can make to world evangelism is to raise up churches that will fulfill their mission to their respective communities. Greater than all other factors for world evangelism, more important than radio, literature, or institutions, as needful as these things are, is the establishment of the Church of Jesus Christ, filled with the Spirit and dedicated to witnessing. Let us establish, by God's help, multitudes of local churches — living cells in the body of Christ (35:11)."

Example of a Church Planter who heard "Opportunity Knocking"

Pastor and Mrs. William Wilson responded to the voice of opportunity and established the Northside Baptist Church, Winnipeg, Manitoba. It is interesting to follow their steps from a large church, First Baptist, Waterloo, Ontario, to the new church in Winnipeg.

Picture a yellow school bus packed with furniture and a family of four, — husband, wife and two sons. This was the setting at a beautiful suburban home in Waterloo, in July 1975. Pastor and Mrs. Wilson had been given a great farewell service the previous Sunday. The 400 member congregation had wished their pastor God's blessing as they prepared to move to Winnipeg to establish a new church.

There was no known interested Christian family or individual with whom the work could be started. However, as the Wilsons looked over the developing subdivision, already with a population of many thousands, and with many more to come, they knew that God would have them establish a church in that area.

The Wilsons and their sons, Neil and Darrell, began to deliver leaflets in the community informing the residents of the beginning of a church with a Sunday School. Pastor Wilson and Neil next began door to door visitation inviting people to the first service. Many visits were made with little indication of interest on the part of any who were contacted. However, the first service was held on Sunday, September 21, 1975. On that morning the pastor drove the bus and his son Neil acted as bus captain. There were 4 adults and 8 children who came to the first service. These with the pastor and his family gave a total attendance of 16. All met together in a school gymnasium that first Sunday. The second Sunday there were again 4 adults but the number of children grew to 14, so the total attendance was 22. The Sunday School met in the large school gymnasium and the 4 adults had a Bible study in the smaller school gymnasium.

The attendance continued to grow at a steady rate. Twenty months later the services were running around the 100 mark, thanks to the consistent visitation work of Pastor and Mrs. Wilson and their family.

In reality, the Wilsons made the church a family project. Pastor Wilson condicted the services in the smaller gymnasium and Mrs. Wilson played the piano. In the other gymnasium their 17 year old son, Neil, led the children's services. Darrell, 12 years old, was the usher and took care of putting out the outdoor sign announcing the services, setting up chairs and equipment. The pastor's oldest son, Rod, and his wife, Merle, who while attending Portage Avenue Baptist Church, Winnipeg, became aware of the great missionary challenge of the new and rapidly developing Maples area. They volunteered for service and soon were in the work with Merle as one of the first Sunday School teachers and Rod as bus driver and mechanic. This family took to heart the words of Donald MacNair" "If the minister and his wife properly supervise this natural involvement, their children will feel more awareness of God at work in His creation, than almost any other children of the church. This is one of the greatest blessings any Christian could ask for his children (48:67)."

The Maples community chosen by the Wilsons was not a typical Anglo-Saxon area. Rather, there was a major concentration of ethnic central Europeans. In addition there was a large East Indian population. As a result, many of the converts came from a Roman Catholic or Hindu background.

The church continues to grow today, not so much by Christians moving in and uniting with the young church, as through personal evangelism and door to door visitation. One can only commend the Wilsons for their vision, zeal, faith and dedication. Today, they look back with praise to God for His faithfulness.

This is one example of many of the potential opportunities on our continent today. We need to heed the Word of the Lord, when he said: "Say not ye, there are yet four months, and then cometh harvest? Behold, I say unto you, lift up your eyes, and look on the fields; for they are white already to harvest (John 4:35)."

Chapter 3

Meadowvale Baptist Church
Mississauga, Ontario

PICKING THE PLACES

Opportunities for the establishment of new churches are unlimited. Calls come to the offices of denominational home secretaries on a routine basis. Since it is not possible to enter all the fields that call for help at the same time, criteria must be set up to help leaders establish priorities. By answering the following questions, the church should be able to discern which one of several communities should be entered first.

I. Is There a Spiritual Vacuum?

This would be the case in a community where there are only liberal and/or holiness churches. These churches do not meet the needs of those who desire an independent, congregational local church structure. Now "There is a difference between communities that 'could use' a conservative Baptist church... and a community that definitely and desperately needs one (100:1)". This type of community needs a Bible believing church for the preaching of the gospel and to give believers an opportunity to become involved in an outreach ministry. Such an area would find a church planter ploughing new ground without fear of building on another man's foundation or of competing with other churches of a similar nature.

An illustration of this is Wabush-Labrador City, Labrador. These twin mining communities were opened in 1958 and 1963.

The 20,000 population was serviced by old line denominations and two holiness groups. Clearly the churches were not able to minister to the type of people one would find in fundamental Baptist churches. Three families desired such a fellowship and deserved the help that was extended. In less than four years, a fine building has been erected on a choice site; the church is organized and functioning. A number have come to experience the saving grace of our Lord through the Labrador West Baptist Church. In fact, this church has called as pastor, Dick Neufeld, who was formerly manager of the Labrador Railroad. Dick lost his position due to alcohol. He was gloriously saved. Following his studies at Nipawin Memorial Bible Institute he accepted the call back to the very city which he had left several years earlier, but this time, like the Apostle Paul, his goal was to preach Christ.

II. Are There Several Families in the Community Praying for a Church?

It helps when there are several believers who are committed to the establishment of a new church. These believers must have a real burden for the lost community and be willing to put their heart and soul into the work. It is one thing to have a desire but it is another matter to be ready to give and work and pray for the new church.

This is the way Grace Baptist Church, Charlottetown, Prince Edward Island, got underway. Four families unburdened their souls to the Fellowship Baptist Home Mission Board and indicated what they were willing to do in order to get assistance for the new church. Their vitality and commitment led to the call of Pastor Alex Rockwell as a church planter. Coming in November, 1973, God used His servant to bring excellent growth. One year later the congregation had grown to 170. Early in 1975 the offerings were running as high as $700.00 a Sunday and in 1976 over $1,000.00 a week. There have been many conversions and baptisms. Today the church has erected a large edifice on a choice ten acre site. It is noteworthy that this growth took place in a city where the housing starts have been limited.

III. Is Land Available?

Although this is not the most important aspect it does have a bearing on church planting. A suitable site with a large sign indicating a church building will be erected can assist in stabilizing aa new work. It is also a testimony to the community.

Purchasing land ahead of time can save considerably on the ultimate cost. At the same time it assists denominational leaders in preparing their plans for the starting of new works. In the fall of 1976 the Fellowship Baptist Home Mission Board purchased a five acre site in Amherstview, Ontario, for $40,000.00. Today, the land is worth twice that. Due to the purchase of property a church is now planned for the area.

IV. Are there other Bible Believing Churches in the Community?

Since there are so many opportunities to settle in areas where there is an absence of Bible believing churches, it is not wise or necessary to move in and crowd another Evangelical pastor. L. P. Waterman suggests that there must be clear-cut evidence from a survey and evaluation that the community definitely needs a conservative Baptist church.

This evidence varies in different sections of the country. If the new church will be stepping on the toes of other sound witnesses or if it will be a case of merely swapping members with one another then the need is not clear-cut. This must be determined by the context of the local situation (108:21).

Bradford, Ontario, with a population of 6,500 plus several thousands in Bond Head, Beaton and Holland Landing lacked such a witness. In a study of the area no Evangelical church, as such, was found. It was easy for the Fellowship Baptists to see that a church was needed in this area. Their judgment was correct. Pastor James Rendle moved to the community, February 1, 1977. By Christmas of the same year, the church had purchased two choice acres and the attendance was near the 100 mark.

V. Is the Population Large enough to Support a Church?

The aim is to start new churches that have the potential for self-support within a maximum of five years. Smaller communities should not, however, be neglected. Perhaps this is where a strong self-supporting church might use Theological Education by Extension to train laymen to go and minister to small communities. Fellowship Baptists have several courses available for pastors desiring to train their laymen. Courses included are: Book of Mark, Homiletics, and Church planting. Future courses will include: Old Testament Survey, New Testament Survey, Romans and a course on Doctrine.

VI. Is there a Pastor
With a Burden for
a Specific Community?

This was the situation when Fellowship Baptists entered Port Hope, Ontario. Pastor Joe MacDonald had such a burden for the city. He made this need known. Sensing God's direction in his life, and because of his willingness to launch out, this city had a priority over other cities, for Fellowship Baptists in 1975.

Today the church has purchased a former legion hall which has been beautifully renovated. The church has ample space with excellent off-street parking. The auditorium will handle a congregation of 135. The total cost was $60,000.00. This is the first stage. The second will include the purchase of a campus site and the erection of a major building complex.

VII. Has the Community been Prepared?

Often a church will hold Vacation Bible Schools for one or two summers before launching a new work. Backyard Bible clubs, musical rallies and visitation work can assist in preparing a field. A number of churches have operated a bus ministry until the area was ready for a church. Harold L. Longenecker suggests:

Have you any means of contact with the people? This may be a determining consideration. If we are faced with two openings, not knowing which to enter, we would probably be wise, all other things being equal, to enter the field with which some contact has been established. Sometimes a friend or relative can help acquaint us with a needy area, or an individual in one community may have friends in a more distant place where spiritual needs exists (44:40)."

VIII. Is the City a Key Centre?

Is the city the capital of a province or state? Is it a county site where political decisions are made? Is it going to face rapid growth which will make it a key centre in the next decade.

Fellowship Baptist Home Missions, in seeking to strengthen the Trans-Canada Fellowship, placed Regina, Saskatchewan, as a priority city in 1974. This provincial capital is undergoing major development. It was a wise decision as the church has now secured an excellent two acre site and the new edifice is slated for completion in 1978. Pastor Arthur Birch is the church planter in Regina.

IX. Is the Holy Spirit Leading to a Particular Area?

The Spirit of God speaks to us, quietly, confirming our decisions. This is especially true in church planting. One should wait upon the Lord to sense if the area is spiritually ripe for such a project. As L. P. Waterman suggests: "It takes discernment to see and evaluate the ripeness of a community, but it is not difficult to discern if our heart, eyes and ears are open. Prayer has a real vital part in this discernment (108:21)."

Example of a Church Planter Who Knows how to Pick Sites

Few pastors have had the experience of William L. Hiltz who has founded five churches in a fifteen year period. Each church is located on an excellent site and each is in a growing situation today.

It was a cold day in January, 1957 when Pastor Hiltz met with a few people in North Bay, Ontario. The city, known as "The Gateway to the North" had only one other Baptist church to serve a population of over 20,000. The projections for growth indicated the population would double in the 60's and double again in the 70's. If ever a city was ripe for a fundamental Baptist church, North Bay was it.

Pastor Hiltz had a five year church planting ministry in North Bay. Being a northern community, many residents were transients. This meant the church's influence spread to many other places. Scores of people who, having been reached, have moved on to be witnesses for Christ and have been used of the Lord to encourage churches in other cities.

Following North Bay, Pastor Hiltz took up the church planting work at Alta Vista Baptist Church, Ottawa, Ontario. Actually the work had the benefit of three previous pastors who has a part in founding the church. Upon the arrival of Bill Hiltz, the congregation made a serious effort to move out of the school, where their services were held, into a building program. Within a year a large edifice with fine Sunday School rooms was built. This enabled the congregation to expand even more.

The Ottawa site of the Alta Vista Church was chosen due to the large expanding development of the community and the lack of other fundamental churches in the area. The site was of ample size and the congregation has since doubled the over all space of the building.

Three years later Bill Hiltz responded to the developing area of Bramalea City. This was to be a planned city with a central commerce area and select industrial belts to support the residents. The maximum population was planned in the overall picture of the size of the city. Up to this point there was no other Baptist church in the city. Upon Bill's arrival in October, 1965, the core of Christians were meeting in a school for Sunday services.

Two years earlier the Fellowship Home Mission Board had purchased a church site but held it in trust for the launching of a church. To aid in the starting of the work, the board also purchased a portable unit which was used for 18 months by the Bramalea Church.

The church continued to grow and before long a trade was made and the original site was exchanged for a tremendous six acre site, across from one of the largest shopping malls in Canada. The site alone is valued at over one half million dollars. Upon the resignation of Bill Hiltz, Pastor Stuart Silvester was called by the church. Attendance now exceeds 700 with another building program planned to double the present auditorium in order to provide seating for 1500.

In the latter part of 1969 there were four families who were members of Kenmuir Baptist Church, Port Credit, Ontario. The families were concerned about the expanding area in the western part of Mississauga, which is the fastest growing community in Canada. With the support of the parent church Bible studies were held and regular Sunday services were conducted in a school. Before long the small group called Bill Hiltz to be their pastor.

Within the first year he led the group to purchase a two acre site for $50,000. through the assistance of the Inter-Church Planning Association. Although the actual value was $200,000. the Association worked with the developers to reduce the total cost of the property. The excellent site is located on the main thoroughfare of Erin Mills, across from the recreation centre and one block from the regional high school. The church is well established today and completed their edifice in 1978.

Opening services for the Meadowvale Bible Baptist Church were held on April 30, 1972. Two years later the congregation was offered by the Fellowship Home Mission Board a two acre site in the Meadowvale West area. Strategically located, the site was enlarged by the church securing an adjoining day-care centre site.

The initial building which opened in March, 1978, provides for worship and educational facilities for about 300 people. It also houses a Christian day nursery with a variety of early childhood education programs. The school was in such demand that parents had their children enrolled a year before the building was ready.

The building, in its design stage, was approved by the Provincial Government of Ontario licensing authorities to provide for 160 children at a time. The demand of the community soon filled the school to capacity. The $325,000 building is only phase one in a series of planned facilities for the church.

Plans call for the purchase of a three acre site, located across from the Town-Centre, and just three blocks from the church, for the erection of a Christian senior citizens residence. For this and other enterprises, Bill Hiltz has envisioned a large team of workers, laboring together in this rapidly growing community.

Bill Hiltz was asked how he established priorities when there were so many opportunities. He replied that it was in God's sovereign grace, he picked the communities and the sites. The Lord put the burden on his heart for each of the five locations.

He believes the important criterion for setting one community ahead of another is the call of God. In each of the five situations mentioned, there was a need because of a greatly expanding population. There was a present need because of people already in the area, and research showed in each case, that there would be large numbers of new people during the years immediately ahead. In most of the situations this meant not just thousands but tens of thousands of people.

We know that the message of the gospel is addressed to people. Thus churches must be established where people are and, in turn, where you know they will be. It is best to get in on the ground floor, better to reach people as they move into an area.

How did Bill Hiltz go about finding sites? He would check out, and spend weeks doing so, every means possible in seeing what land was available. He drove around looking for "For Sale" signs. He would talk with real estate agents. He would find strategically located vacant land, and search out the owner to see if and when it would be available. He talked with developers in different areas. It has been his experience that they were friendly and most co-operative.

What changes would he make in the sites chosen? If possible, he would buy larger acreage.

"Picking the Places" is an important part of the ministry of church planting. The earlier you do it, the better it is. It is not likely that land in an expanding area will decrease in value. Seek the face of God for direction. Look up realtors. Get your church planted not only on a rock but on solid ground!

Chapter 4

WHERE THERE'S A WILL, THERE'S A WAY

Each church has its own unique beginning. There are as many ways of starting new churches as there are churches. However, there are three main methods: Pioneer, Partnership and Parent-Daughter church planting.

I. The Pioneer Method

Where the pioneer method is used, a denomination's home mission board will provide full or partial support in order that a new church may be launched by a church planter in a given community. This is usually carried out where the denomination does not have churches near at hand to assist. This was the case when the Fellowship Baptist Home Mission Board started the Labrador West Baptist Church in Wabush, Labrador. The nearest Baptist church was over two hundred miles away in Sept-Iles, Quebec.

One readily appreciates the problems faced while using the Pioneer Method. The isolation factor is a real problem, both for the church planting pastor and the church. There is a ministry of reinforcement when pastors of like mind can meet and fellowship together. The same applies to the church members. When this method is used it is advisable for the denomination to provide funds for guest speakers to frequently visit the new work, upon the invitation of the pastor.

High Park Baptist Church, Toronto, took a personal interest in the Wabush Church. Two deacons from High Park, Jack Gibson and Gordon Stimers, took time to fly to Labrador and spend several days with the pastor and church. This visit was a great help. Deacons of the new church were able to learn from experienced deacons how to assist the pastor. Many areas of misunderstanding were cleared up. Pastor and people appreciated such spiritual reinforcement.

2) Seeking to gain a foothold in the new community presents another problem. The pastor must gain the confidence of civic leaders. Much promotion is needed to acquaint the community with his presence in the area and what he is seeking to do. This is where Vacation Bible Schools and Home Bible Studies help to open homes to a new church.

3) A third problem is a financial one. The national denominational board must carry the heavy financial responsibility until a foothold has been secured. The monthly grant should be large enough to make it possible for the pastor to participate full time, but limited enough to challenge the church to do her part.

Most denominational home mission boards have lived through the frustration of trying to maintain a definite and permanent policy for grants. There needs to be flexibility to the extent where each field is considered individually. The following factors are involved in the grant support:

1. Each group has its own peculiar circumstances that tend to limit or foster growth.
2. Pastors vary from one to another, as to marriage, experience, and family responsibility.
3. The cost of living in a given community might differ greatly from one part of the country to another.
4. Increased mobility of population, due partly to business organizations making wholesale transfers of personnel, can hurt a new church if one or two strong families are involved.

It is wise to have reducing grants spread over a period of time. Dr. H. Taylor Pendley of the Baptist General Convention of Texas gives the following counsel: "One of the greatest mistakes is for the sending church, or board, to withdraw financial support suddenly when the dependent attitude of the mission has been created by the paternal policy of the home body. It is better to work out a plan to reduce the financial support gradually and increase the responsibility of the congregation (97:49)."

II. The Partnership Method

In this case, an association of churches work together to form a new church. It becomes a joint enterprise on behalf of the association. The co-operating churches may share both families and finances. At times, if required, the national denomination home mission board may supplement the financial support of the new church.

This method gives association churches a project that serves to motivate their members in mission giving. It can encourage the supporting churches in fostering their own growth. It is a testimony of what churches can do when they work together.

There are problems that surface at times with this Partnership Method. One is the strain if and when families are on loan to the new church. It is hard to cut ties with the parent church during the time the families are working in the new field. Again it is often a difficult period when the families return to their home church, as the new church may resent their departure. There is a feeling at times that they should stand by the new work until it is even stronger. The question here is, — How strong should the new church be before the families on loan be permitted to return to their home church?

Another problem stems from the amount of support offered by the association churches. There are those who willingly give of their finances and members. There are others who are willing to stand by and let them give. All churches should be equally involved, as the need arises, in the planting of new churches.

Still another problem is faced by the founding pastor. He is under obligation to work with the sister churches, and rightly so. He does not have the same freedom that perhaps he would like to have in his work.

III. The Parent-Daughter Method

Without question, this is the best way. Just as a mother gives birth to a child, so a church gives birth to a new church. It is the best method because the support and experience of a stronger church are available to the new work.

Using this method, the parent church commissions several families to launch a new church several miles from the parent work. This is done by taking a survey of church families and finding clusters in a needy area. This survey is carried out with the prayerful support of the church seeking the will of God for an outreach ministry. The survey should include possible meeting places and available sites for the future church.

After the facts are sorted out a full presentation is made to the church. A vote is taken and once it has been approved, a challenge is extended to interested families to become involved in this evangelistic outreach. It is best if from one to three deacons can be involved in the new work to help provide leadership and stability. As soon as there is a nucleus of believers committed to the establishment of this new church, they may be formally commissioned by the parent church. A pastor should then be called to give direction to the new work. It is best to have the pastor called jointly by the church and the families planning to commence the new work.

The new pastor will often serve on the staff of the parent church for the first few months. Combined evening services with the parent church presents an opportunity to include reports on visitation, building progress, attendances and other activities to the mother church. It tends to excite both the parent and daughter churches and motivate both in their own ministry. One youth group will often serve the two churches. Gradually the new work takes on more services until it has reached the point where it is able to carry the full responsibility for its services.

At times the parent church will provide a deacon who acts as a liaison between the two churches. Communication is important in the first months.

There are several ways to deal with the question of church membership in a new work. Some like to have members of the new work received into the membership of the parent church. In this way they are under the discipline and guidance of a spiritually mature church. Others like to form their own membership from the start. There have been cases when the members of the parent church working with the new work have retained their home membership until the new work is strong. At the same time the new work receives into the membership her own members apart from those from the parent church. It is wise for the new church to organize her membership as soon as possible.

There is often a question concerning the time when a new church may start to observe the ordinances of baptism and the Lord's Supper. Baptism may be administered by the church planting pastor in anticipation of the church organization. The Lord's Supper may be observed as soon as the church is organized.

In his book on starting a daughter church, Donald Benson gives four reasons why such an enterprise should be undertaken:

1. It is God's plan
2. It reaches a new area with the gospel.
3. It revives the mother church.
4. It trains the members of the mother church.

Paul Benjamin gives encouragement for fostering daughter churches:

> *In order to disciple the growing millions living in urban areas an increasing number of congregations must become interested in motherhood. A congregation whose leadership is sold on planting new congregations can be the mother and grandmother of dozens of congregations. Such an attitude requires a great deal of soul searching by members of the mothering congregation.*
>
> *As a staying member of a congregation it may not be easy to watch several families leave on a given Sunday in order to establish a new congregation in a strategic part of the city. Those who are leaving are probably among the top giving members of the congregation both in time and treasure. They may represent a sizeable block of current leadership in the congregation. Others will need to pick up the congregational responsibilities which those who are leaving have laid down in their former congregation.*
>
> *On the other hand it is usually not easy for those who are leaving. Across the years they may have formed vital and active friendships with many members of their previous congregations. Perhaps they have given liberally towards the erection of a commodious house of worship and they must now think in terms of giving generously for the same cause. They may have enjoyed a position of leadership which may now be used in the levelling process of a new daughter congregation.*
>
> *The cause of leaving, however, is often more than compensated for by the joy of pioneering. Charter members of a new congregation often point with pride and thankfulness to the picture of a handful of people who struggled a few years before to start a new congregation. Then they look at the current attendance board which shows how their efforts have been multiplied. Many of them have performed functions of Christian service in the new congregation because of necessity which they never dreamed they could do. It is also interesting to note the rise of latent leadership in the mothering congregations. With many former congregational leadership posts now vacant former sitting type members move into worker roles (6:46).*

There are several problems with this Parent-Daughter
method. One is timing. In a sense this is a problem with most
enterprises. Getting started is often half the battle. It is easy to
postpone. There is no problem in suggesting that First Church
start a new work in two or three years. As long as you keep it in
the future there are no real problems to face. The struggle comes
when you establish a time-table that is imminent. Some members
may offer opposition and seek to postpone action. Thorough
preparation can avoid this issue to some degree.

The leadership of the sponsoring church is often zealous to
guard the membership. There is no merit in giving to a new
work, members who have been inactive. It is harder to yield
steady members who have been tithers and workers. You often
hear the remark: "What would our church do without those
families?" In fact, for many churches this is the real problem. I
recall one deacon telling me that their church could not afford to
give up any members for a new work. This particular church was
packed to the doors with several hundreds of people. Yet dozens
of people were simply filling eighteen inches of space in a pew
Sunday morning. The church had no debt. How do you respond
to such a remark? The answer is to emphasize that it is not my
church or our church, but His church. What is the will of God in
this matter? What would God have you do about starting a new
church? As God gave us His Son, so should we be willing to share
families with another community, in order to start a new work.

Local provincialism is another problem that often must be
faced. Pastor L.P. Waterman, who is the New Church Co-
ordinator for the Conservative Baptist Home Mission Society,
gives the following little ditty which well portrays local
provincialism:

> **To plant a church across the state,**
> **O, that will be glory;**
> **But to start one in the town nearby,**
> **Well...that's another story!**

He goes on to suggest:

> *Local provincialism in reverse is the other side of the*
> *provincial coin. It is a sort of state provincialism in reverse.*
> *An attitude of local provincialism may favor and even*
> *support financially, state, national and foreign church*
> *planting. However, for several possible reasons, local*
> *provincialism balks at considering the local communities*
> *surrounding the church as a mission field. This attitude may*
> *prevail even though families are coming to the church from*

these other local communities. The fact that there is a clear cut need in at least one of these surrounding areas may not even put a dent in the attitude of local provincialism.

Local provincialism seems to say: 'Why bother starting a new church when you can abide under the wings of our existing programs, facilities, and organization?' Other reasons for local provincialism may be a fleshly desire to build an 'empire' locally at the expense of evangelizing the surrounding communities. Believers will travel great distances to church. So will those who have a loyalty to a building and those who do not care to be much more than attenders. Fear of 'losing' families or loss of prestige bolster the bottleneck of local provincialism. Since the congregation is totally unaware of the local mission field because of a silence from the leadership, laymen do not seem concerned over the fact that they cannot get many of their unsaved neighbours or even newly saved friends to go to another town to church. Mere mention of a local divide and multiply possibility brings an unpleasant stir in the church. We trust that it doesn't take something like the great persecution in Acts 8 to break this bottleneck. A local provincialism could not afford to lose a Paul or a Barnabas from the church at Antioch (10:1-5).

A parent church that encourages families to launch a new work usually fills up again. Temple Baptist Church, Sarnia, Ontario, commissioned fifty members to launch Huron Baptist Church in 1974. Temple Baptist Church is now filled to capacity under the leadership of Pastor Lambert Baptist, while the new Huron Baptist Church has attendances exceeding 200. A few months ago the Huron Church dedicated a new $250,000 edifice. This is the way it usually goes. Now Temple Baptist is planning another new work with the same sense of stewardship and support.

An interesting remark was made recently in the fellowship hour at Victory Baptist Church, Newmarket, Ontario. This church had just sponsored a new work in Bradford, Ontario. Six months later, Ron Hartwick, chairman of the deacons, told me that their attendances were up and the offerings were running over $100 more since the new work started. This appears to be the pattern experienced time after time. As Paul Benjamin states: "It has been shown repeatedly that planting new congregations does not usually deter the growth of the mothering congregation. In fact in many instances a consistent policy of planting new congregations has increased the concern for the

Kingdom by the existing congregation to the point that its growth rate has actually increased (6:48)."

M. Wendell Belew writes: "It is often noted that one church (local) which has divided into two churches will each produce as great growth as the original."

IV. Preparing a Field for a New Church

There are several ways of preparing a community for a new church. Some churches like to cultivate a field for a year or two. One summer a Vacation Bible School can be conducted in the community in question. This may be followed up with a series of back yard Bible Clubs in the Fall. A weekly Home Bible Study is often held involving one or more families from the new community. This presents a fine opportunity for several families to open their homes and to indicate their degree of interest and possible future involvement in a new work. An occasional rally with a feature speaker or musical group helps prepare the field. A survey is often used to give some indication of the people residing in the community.

It is wise to have a series of prayer meetings for the founding families. This presents the opportunity for families to know if God is indeed leading them to start a new church. It answers a number of questions concerning leadership and involvement in the new church.

The Fellowship Baptist Home Mission Board has introduced a pilot project of Theological Education by Extension. It has been well received and is being introduced across the nation. The purpose is to train laymen who in turn will open new areas for church extension. One pastor has several men in his church taking courses. There are three towns within thirty miles of his church building where new churches are needed. His thought is to use his men to launch these churches. This is vision!

Example of a Pastor Who Knows
How to Plant Daughter Churches

One of the finest examples of the Daughter Church precept is that of Cloverdale Baptist Church, Surrey, British Columbia. Pastor Ian Bowie gave excellent leadership in fostering this ministry at Cloverdale.

The church was founded in 1931. It is not a large church. The membership is about 175 with the Sunday School attendance running between 275 and 300. The church has experienced real growth under the leadership of Pastor Bowie. In 1969, the membership was 81 while the Sunday School averaged in the 160's. Since 1969 the church has grown from 10 to 15% each year.

This church, in its 45 years of service, has fostered five daughter churches. Her pastor in 1949 was Lloyd Jackson. He was used of God to lead the church in its first daughter church outreach. In Northwest Langley, a tiny struggling missionary Baptist church was facing extinction. Pastor Jackson and Cloverdale congregation took over this infant work. And what of the Langley Church today? It has recently erected a fine new building on a 2½ acre site.

In 1955 Pastor John Stewart served the Cloverdale Church. In that Fall, Mr. and Mrs. Glen Redline, members of the church, gave leadership in the planting of their second work, North Delta Baptist Church. This became a joint venture both of Ladner and Cloverdale Baptist Churches. Pastor Stan Braunberger has seen this congregation surge ahead. Plans are underway for a major building expansion in the near future.

John Steward was pastor of Cloverdale for thirteen years. During this time he led the church to foster a third work in the small but developing Fraser Valley community of Aldergrove. Preparation was made for the work by providing transportation to and from Aldergrove for Sunday School. Patricia Mission, associated with the Baptist General Conference, merged with the group going to Cloverdale from Aldergrove in order to form what is today the Aldergrove Baptist Church. Today it is a strong work under the leadership of Pastor Rod Wilkinson and has just completed a major building program.

In 1973 several families from Cloverdale, North Delta and Faith Baptist Church, Vancouver met together in the living room of Mrs. Norma Reeve to pray for the establishment of a work in the Newton area of Surrey. Today, Pastor John Greb, with his wife Pat, give able leadership in this developing community of 18,000. Mrs. Greb has opened a day-care ministry which has proved fruitful for the church. In 1975 the church itself won the national Sunday School contest sponsored by the Church Ministries Board of the Fellowship Baptist Churches in Canada.

The fifth daughter church was begun in North Surrey in November of 1974. A fine 2½ acre site was purchased for $67,000 complete with an edifice seating 160.

Pastor Ian Bowie has come to the following conclusions through the experience of planting daughter churches:

1. A church can participate in the planting of a new church.
2. A church can grow while participating in the planting of a new church.
3. A church can have an effective ministry while participating in church planting.

Is it worthwhile to foster daughter works? The answer is a resounding Yes! It really staggers the imagination when one considers the ultimate potential. Yes, "Where There's a Will, There's a Way!"

Chapter 5

MEN, NOT MACHINERY

Without a leader, church planting will not take place. Elmer Towns has well said: "God still uses a man. One of the greatest tasks a man can do today is to start a church (72:12)." Pastor George Bell reminds his students at Central Baptist Seminary, Toronto, that God uses men, not machinery. When God has a task to be done, He begins with a man who, under God, serves as a leader. See Judges 2:15,16; 3:9; 3:15; 3:21; 4:4; 6:11; 10:3; 11:1 and 13:24. This emphasis causes us to consider the fact that the church planter is the key to church planting. There are several reasons why this is so.

I. His Call from God Confirms the Work He Must Do

No pastor should take up church planting unless he is sure this is what God wants him to do. Just as God calls to a specific self-supporting church, so God calls to the special field of establishing a new church. Elmer Towns says it so well: "The most important factor in beginning a new church is its conception in the mind of God's man who is motivated by the Holy Spirit. The foundation of a new church requires a man called of God. If a man is going to start a successful church he must be fully confident that God has led him to do so. The heartaches, pressures and hard work required in starting a church demand that the pastor have the assurance of the call of God (73:128,129)." George Bell gives as one of the essential qualities of a church planter, a man who has a conviction that he is God-called, God-appointed and God-directed. He knows he's saved and called to preach in general and he has a particular call to a particular community.

II. His Call from Founding Members Reaffirms The Call of God

His call from the founding members manifests his key post of leadership. The members have seen the way he is starting and sense the fact that their leader knows where he is going and are ready to support him in that work. It is a great privilege to be called by a group of believers to lead them in the work of the ministry. In so many words, the members are saying to their church planter, "We have confidence in your leadership, we believe in your objectives, we recognize your call from God, and we are ready to work with you."

III. His Training has Prepared him for His Work

The church planter will take time to discipline himself through study. Nothing can take the place of a consistent application to good books. It is most profitable to be subject to the influence of various teachers who are knowledgeable in their fields. The fruit of his studies is seen as he applies the theories to his practice.

IV. His Talents are suited for The Work

The man God calls, God has prepared and equipped. It is not every man who can be a church planter. Rather, a man ascertains the gifts needed by a church planter, including physical strength, ability to endure long hours, and carry out an extensive and active ministry of confronting people, especially strangers, with the Word of God. He considers his own talents as well as the gifts of his wife. Recognizing that God has ordained him for this special work, he is ready to dedicate his body and gifts to it. If God calls a man God will have him ready for this work. No man should shy away because he does not have all the gifts he would desire to have for such a ministry. In the final analysis, God takes ordinary men, develops their natural gifts and works through them.

Is there a personality type that is more successful than others in starting churches? Elmer Towns gives the following answer:

Some think that the church planter must be the rugged individualist who can persevere in spite of the odds. Others think he must be a charismatic personality by collecting people to himself hence building the church on his own charm. From my observation I have seen all types of men build churches. Bill Munroe who founded the Florence Baptist Temple was shy in meeting people yet aggressive in doing the work of God. So was Carl Godwin in Lincoln, Nebraska. Ruy Holland is the unstoppable force who can follow through the immovable object with love. Bud Calvert is sophisticated and would be at home with the executive. Each builder of churches has his own strength and weaknesses. Other men begin churches in rural areas with a dogged determination that attracts the rugged farmer.

Since Jesus is the founder of the Church He uses human channels who are dedicated to Him. Only God can accentuate a man's talents while at the same time compensating his weaknesses. God uses the inadequate individual with meagre abilities and marginal equipment to serve in limited circumstances. When he is God's man he beats insurmountable odds, overcoming oppressive obstacles to accomplish a work of God (73:158).

V. His Time is Wholly Given to Church Planting

He sleeps, eats and works 24 hours a day living with the concept of a church. His members and officers are involved in services and committees but there is nothing like the involvement of a pastor who has given everything he has to see a church born. He will budget his time to guard against things that might take away from his main work. He will rise early in the morning and will not be afraid to visit in the evenings.

VI. Difference Between a Church Planter And a Regular Pastor

There is a real difference both in the emphasis of the work and the matter of authority.

The pastor of a self-supporting church accepts a call and as such must carry on the regular routine of services, visiting the members and, so to speak, keeping the wheels turning. Whereas a pioneer pastor can emphasize leadership in organizing the work according to his understanding of the New Testament. He can devote much more time to the unsaved. He is not simply building on the foundation of another man.

The pastor of a self-supporting church is expected to keep in line with his board and, to a point, not rock the church. He is the servant of the established church and reports to the same. The pioneer pastor, in gathering new families around him, usually has much more liberty to carry out his plans and to fulfill his vision.

Elmer Towns states well the relationship of pastor and deacons, which applies to pastors serving self-supporting churches as well as to church planters:

> *Some churches regulate to the pastor only the spiritual duties of preaching, teaching and counseling. The fiscal and business matters are handled by deacons or the Board. Such an approach to church administrators is not biblical nor is it practical. Not one verse of scripture supports a deacon run church. Their primary duty is service to the cause of Christ not a legislative body to determine church policy. The criticism is often heard, 'We do not want the pastor to dictate.' I have seen worse dictatorial control of churches by deacons than I have ever seen by a pastor. The pastor is the leader. The deacons or board of laymen serve the cause of Christ and give support (advice to the pastor in carrying out the ministry). The congregation is the final seat of authority to determine policy, direction, and discipline. Hence the church is a faithful system of checks and balances, the pastor, the deacons and the congregation. Each depending on the other while mutually supporting one another in the biblical task before them (72:173).*

Robert Schuller confirms the above with his philosophy of leadership.

> *Any dynamic, progressive and enthusiastic pastor will find his style being cramped, his energy draining away and his dreams turning into despair if he thinks he has to sell his plans and his dreams to a negative thinking congregation. If I were a capitalist financing an enterprise I would insist that the unchallenged leadership be placed in the hands of fulltime thinkers and planners. As a pastor heading up a church I insist on the same.*
> *Let there be no dodging on this issue. Pastor, do you hear me? You should be the spark plug. You should be the inspiring commander leading the troops up the hill.*
> *As president of a corporation and chairman of the board I,,*

a senior minister, am an ex-officio member of all committees (67:53).

VII. Is the Age and Experience of a Pastor a Deciding Factor?

The question is often asked about the age factor of a church planter, as well as his experience. Actually, the Lord has seen fit to use a man fresh out of Bible college or seminary and a retired pastor — to establish churches. The age of a man is not the deciding factor. As Elmer Towns says: "The answer lies not in age or experience but in strategy. . . a preconceived idea of how they would begin a church (73:129,130)." There's a biblical principle to be applied here. Paul suggests in 1 Cor. 1:26-31 that the man whom God calls, God will use. Depending on age and experience alone is not enough for a church planter. Does he have a call from God? Does he know where he is going? Does he have gifts to carry through his plan? These are the deciding factors and are more important than age or even experience.

Two Examples of Church Planters

One December morning in 1972, twenty-three year old John Kenyon asked to see me. He had just graduated from Emmanuel Bible College, Kitchener, Ontario. Possibly due to his age he was impatient to receive a pastorate. It was either a secular job or perhaps, under home missions, start a new church. He would have no problem obtaining employment but he felt constrained to the ministry. This was the call of God to him.

Sensing his burden to do the will of God I suggested that he go out and start his own church. In response to his question where he might start, I mentioned the name of a high school teacher in Alliston, Ontario, who was interested in seeing a Bible-believing church in his community. "See what you can do," I said, "and when you have several families call me and I'll seek help for you from Fellowship Baptist Home Missions."

Two months later John Kenyon called inviting me to meet with several families from the Allison community. It was a real joy to go up on a cold wintry night in February, 1973, and there find a group of about twenty people, meeting for information and direction. Within two years the Grace Baptist Church was running around 125 in attendance and $700 in weekly offerings. The church received financial support for 24 months before it became self-supporting. A fine site was purchased on the main thoroughfare and a functional building has been renovated to serve the young church.

If God spares you to the retiring age of 65 you may want to get out your easy chair and sit back and watch the action. This was not the case with Gordon Searle who was 68 when he responded to the call of Fellowship Baptist Home Missions to lead in the formation of a new church in Cornwall, Ontario. A group of 29 people had just severed relationships with their church over a matter of church policy. Doctrine did not enter into the situation. As a result the parting was much more taxing. The new church would need the warm heart of a man of God. Gordon Searle was just the individual. In addition his wife Hazel through the years has been a model pastor's wife. Together, they were able to pour oil on wounds, rescue a group of people and form them into a fine church. Gordon Searle explains it this way: "My congregation was 'a hurting church'. Some of the families were divided by the split forced by the former pastor. Much of my time was spent in a healing ministry among the flock and in visiting the visitors. We had to be very careful for many in the city did not understand the division and the other church was very bitter. Their bitterness was quite vocal and they had nothing good to say for those who had formerly been the backbone of their church."

Within 24 months this new church had become self-supporting. Today the church has purchased a fine twenty acre site and a large building is underway.

These two brief case histories are cited to illustrate that there is a place for a young man, fresh out of school, and for pastors who are retired. The latter can have an extended ministry. The attitude of a pastor's heart and his determination to get started and to do a work is of more value than the age factor.

John Kenyon in response to the question concerning the advantages in using a man just out of school, replied, giving two good advantages:

1. Such a man has lots of enthusiasm.
2. He is not locked into a set 'how you do it' pattern.

He lists the following disadvantages.

1. Obvious lack of experience in preaching, administration, visitation and general pastoral work is a hindrance.
2. There is a feeling of inadequacy in carrying out certain functions.
3. There is a lack of doctrinal solidity, that is, he is still thinking things through.
4. Then there is a possible inferiority complex due to age and lack of experience.

Gordon Searle, in response to the question as to the advantages in using men of retirement age, replied: "I have always said we should not send young graduates to do pioneer work. On the contrary we do well to send mature men. Men of retirement age have met almost every situation that can possibly arise. They have learned by trial and error how to deal with these problems. They are not so easily discouraged when things get tough. I am sure that many young men have left the ministry because they became discouraged due to 'the heaviness of the way'. Some of these were well trained but maybe not so well conditioned. Older men do not have as much to lose and maybe a bit more to give."

William F. Lee, chairman of the New Church Development Committee for the St. Johns Presbytery in Orlando, Florida, gives the following advantages of using retired pastors as church planters.

1. It gives the freedom to fail because he has his victories behind him, and so is not as personally and emotionally tied to the success of the congregation.
2. It is less expensive as the retired pastor has the benefit of old age pensions.
3. It secures better leadership.
4. It gives the church a chance to select their new pastor after the work is going.

John Kenyon said he would do the following things differently had he the opportunity to do it again.

1. A solid doctrinal statement would be previously prepared.
2. A church constitution would be at least basically outlined.
3. He would have the congregation cemented together into one working body before he developed interest in building an edifice.
4. He would operate as a mission with as few church officers as possible until he knew the people better in the matter of doctrine, gifts, personalities and motivations.
5. He would provide a ministry as family oriented as possible.
6. After the initial opening period of four to six months he would endeavour to get the members to assume as many responsibilities as possible so he could give his time primarily to preaching and pastoral ministries.

Gordon Searle gives the following disadvantages in using older men as church planters.

1. He might overstay his ministry with the new work.
2. It might be difficult for him to relate to all ages, especially the youth.
3. Many older men are inflexible.

It is interesting to mention that when Gordon Searle went to Cornwall, he specifically said it would be for a 24 month period. It is wise to recommend some guidelines as to a time limit in the case of a retired pastor. It should be pointed out that Gordon Searle was able to relate extremely well to the youth of the congregation. They took to him because they sensed his love and concern. He knew how to listen. His home was opened. His heart was big. His smile was broad.

Inflexible? Not Gordon Searle!

Gordon Searle had two additional pastoral experiences since Cornwall. In one letter he closed with the following comments: "I am enjoying my present ministry to the full! My strength is like that of Caleb when he said: 'Give me this mountain'."

A young graduate, a retired pastor — both have a part in church planting. God calls "Men, Not Machinery". The words of Robert H. Schuller are so apt: "There is no substitute for dynamic, agressive, positive, inspiring leadership. Almost without exeption lack of success means the lack of effective leadership. And the reverse is true, great success is the result of great leadership (67:48)."

A final word from Robert H. Schuller makes a fitting climax to this chapter: "Great things will happen in the church where big thinking lay people will say to their pastor, 'pastor we want you to spend all of your time dreaming great dreams and how our church can become the greatest mission for Jesus Christ in this whole territory (68:56)."

Chapter 6

THE LETTER AND THE SPIRIT

You have moved to Maintown, North America. You sense that this is the will of God for you. Certainly, the city you have studied is in need of the work you desire to establish. How do you proceed?

The answer depends somewhat on whether your field has already been cultivated. Are you starting with one or more families or just by yourself? The latter is harder and of course a lonely path. You are there by yourself with just the members of your own family. There is no one to usher people to their seats. There is no one to assist you with the Sunday School. There is no one to count and deposit the offerings in the bank. There is no one to critize your sermons, except your wife! Yes, there are disadvantages.

However, there are some advantages which may not be evident at first. No one is around to say: "We never tried it that way before," which, according to Ralph Neighbour, "are the seven last words of the church (55:15)." Starting with your own family you can build a church according to the New Testament. You are not inheriting a structure that might contain some things that are contrary to your way of thinking and working. Furthermore, you are not inheriting the problems of another pastor; the one who follows you will have that privilege! Of course you have the psychological advantage of knowing that the attendance can only go up. In fact, there's an excitement the first Sunday, 13 in attendance, the second, 19, the third 42, and you are off climbing, week by week. You have a determination to make a "go" of it, for the glory of God.

There are a number of procedures to follow in launching a new work.

I. Secure Suitable Housing

One of the first steps is to secure suitable housing that is comfortable and adequate for your family. Try to locate near the field you want to develop, both to save time and fuel costs and to be available to the people you want to reach for the Lord. The home that you choose should be in keeping with the majority of the folks you are seeking to serve.

II. Suggestive Initial Meeting Places

Your initial meeting place can be almost any shelter that is available. Seek to secure your space well in advance of the opening date of services.

Many churches begin in a home. This certainly follows the New Testament pattern. The pastor or some other family will open their recreation room for services. Interested families will come to a home for Sunday services, whereas less interested folk and those who are comparatively new to the community may not. It is therefore, advisable to plan to meet in a private home only as a temporary arrangement until a suitable "neutral" meeting place can be found.

Many churches have started by renting a Seventh Day Adventist Church building. Here there is no fear of not having the building available for Sunday services! Northside Fellowship Baptist, North Sydney, Nova Scotia, started in May 1974, renting the Seventh Day Church building.

Various types of stores can be utilized. A Christian automobile dealer opened his building for the starting of a new church. Saturday evening he arranged for the cars to be moved out of the large display room. The hallways and offices were used for Sunday School. It soon became known as "the automobile church"! The new church in Moosonee, on the southern shores of James Bay, in Northern Ontario, had its start in a former laundromat.

III. Public Institutions are Available

The Wabush Baptist Church in Labrador, Newfoundland, started in the large recreation centre. The Port of Fellowship Baptist Church, Port Elgin, Ontario, started in the public library. Today, both churches have new buildings.

Centennial Baptist Church, Markham, Ontario, rented an auditorium that can be leased. Developers are open to suggestions about leasing space to organizations.

Lodges and fraternal organizations are usually happy to work with new churches. Bible Baptist Church, Rothesay, New Brunswick started in the O.O.F. lodge building. The Thousand Islands Baptist Church of Brockville, Ontario, rented the Moose Lodge building for several years.

In a number of cities the Roman Catholic Church has been willing to rent their schools for starting new churches. This was the way Fellowship Baptist Church, Cornwall, Ontario, began.

A vacant warehouse was the starting place for Central Baptist Church, Milwaukee, Wisconsin (73:15). Yes, even funeral homes have been used for churches. Such was the case of Calvary Baptist Church, St. Cloud, Minnesota.

The majority of new churches, at some point in their growth, find it necessary to rent public school space. Here you will find many things working in your favour. The class rooms are suitable for Sunday School. The gym can provide good accomodation for church services. It is easy to advertise the name of the school. Generally there is sufficient parking. The cost is often minimal, in fact, in many cities you pay only for the custodian.

IV. Making Yourself Known in the Community

You are now ready to make yourself known in the community. This involves door-to-door visitation seeking to cover every home in the area where your services are being held. Make use of the radio and other media. You will note a later chapter on promotion. Sufficient to say that your visitation is a key for the opening services.

This is the time to arrange for a visitation blitz. You can invite sister churches from your association to share with you and your founding families in a united effort. Friday night and Saturday, preceding the opening Sunday, arrange to visit as many homes as possible. This can be a combined friendship and evangelism call. Prepare an attractive leaflet and leave it at the home along with a gospel tract.

A most successful cooperative visitation blitz was held by Pastor Don Robins at Lower Sackville, Nova Scotia. At a pastor's meeting on October 3, 1975, he shared his plans for launching Temple Baptist Church. Pastors agreed to support his visitation blitz. On a cold weekend in January, 1976, representatives came from Prince Edward Island, New Brunswick, Nova Scotia and Ontario to assist. Over 3000 homes were visited. The people present on the first Sunday came as a result of the visitation blitz. Pastor Robins heartily recommends this as a good way to get your opening services underway.

V. Home Bible Studies and Prayer Services

If you have the joy of starting with one or more families before the opening Sunday, plan a series of home Bible studies and prayer services. This gives you an opportunity to get to know your families. Together you are seeking the will of God about doing a work that is pleasing to Him. You will soon ascertain whether there is a working kinship in the group. Pastor James Rendle of Bradford Baptist Church, Bradford, Ontario, tried this with good success. In fact, from these sessions came five new church deacons.

In these sessions let the people know what you are planning to do. They need to be aware of your convictions. Settle once and for all questions dealing with doctrine and the two ordinances of the church. You should not wait for others to make a decision before you declare your stand. You are the leader and they have a right to know where you are planning to lead them.

VI. Prepare a Statement of Faith and Constitution

With your founding members you will want to draw up a statement of faith. A short-cut is to adopt your denominational statement of faith. It has been carefully drawn up. You can take each section and explain its meaning.

You will need some guidelines for handling business meetings. A simple set of bylaws with a constitution will help. Your constitution should include the name of the church, the purpose of the church, the statement of faith, and affiliation. Your bylaws will state your officers' terms of service as well as the time and order of business sessions.

There are some who oppose having a constitution. It was Dr. T.T. Shields who said that when his church burns down, save everything but the constitution. However, you can have problems without some document to serve as a guide for business sessions. One church, after the pastor had resigned, introduced the new pastor on his closing Sunday. The congregation did not have an opportunity to hear or vote on the new pastor. Due to the objections, the new pastor agreed to a public membership meeting. Meanwhile, he had arranged for several new members to be received, which he could do, because the church had no constitution or bylaws. At the meeting to extend the call, the new pastor was the chairman. He literally railroaded his call and actually succeeded. That church paid a high price for not having a document to guide them in business sessions!

Caution must be taken not to have a constitution that will hinder the work of the church. This can happen when too high a vote is required in calling a pastor or to carry through some other item of business. One church remained without a pastor for three years due to the requirement of an 80% affirmative vote. One small group held up the calling of a pastor. Another problem is that at times a new church can get bogged down with details in drawing up a constitution. Far better to have the main work done ahead of time. Some pastors write sister churches and take the best from their constitutions. Your denominational home office should have a sample of a workable document.

A constitution and bylaws serve as a tool to help a church function efficiently and effectively. The church was not made for the constitution, but the constitution was made for the church.

Pastor Jimmie Sheffield gives three benefits that may be realized in drawing up a church constitution. "One of the greatest is the facilitation of decision-making. A second advantage is that it saves time. The congregation does not have to spend time discussing how a decision should be made. A third benefit is that it provides needed insight into the nature and purpose of a church. Other advantages relate to legal matters. When conflicts involve internal church problems, the courts sometimes use a church's constitution as a means of resolving problems (94:3)."

VII. Charter Members — Who? How? When?

In drawing up your charter membership roll you will want to set an order that will be followed through the history of the church. Have the group select two spiritual men and let each one give his testimony. These men with the pastor can serve as a membership committee interviewing each prospective charter member, whose name is then brought before the church and voted upon. This is a slow procedure. However, it does elevate the worth of church membership. An individual feels he is really uniting with a special group. This is the way it should be. Believers are special people of God and it is a great privilege to unite with a local church. See Appendix 6 for a suggested church charter.

VIII. Organization Meeting

Once you have a membership of eight or more you are ready to organize. It is not wise to delay this organization service. At the same time you will want to be well prepared.

Your charter membership will be made up of founding Christians of whom, some will be new converts. In most communities you will find a number of Christians who will join you and will wish to be included in the charter membership. Naturally, all charter members will concur with your statement of faith, constitution, and bylaws. Much of the future depends upon this charter membership. One cannot be too careful in screening membership.

Some pastors put off calling for an organization meeting waiting for some on the fringe to come forward and take a definite stand for the Lord. To a certain extent this is letting the fringe people control the time schedule of the organization of the church. You need to proceed by declaring your stand. Those affiliating with you will be ready to stand behind you. Actually, many problems can be averted by the pastor taking his stand and providing leadership. Liberals, and undenominational folks will tend to separate and go their own way.

It is hard to put a time-table on organization. However, under regular conditions you should be able to organize within a period of six to twelve months from the date of the opening Sunday services. By that time people know where you are going. They should be prepared to follow and not hinder the work. To prolong this step beyond reason can hinder the church's growth. A suggested organization service will be found in Appendix 4.

Following the organization the group is now ready to call a pastor. Usually the founder is prepared to accept a call. The treasurer and clerk should also be elected officially, along with those men who will serve with the pastor and deacons. This should lead to definite action regarding the remuneration of the pastor and other details relative to the ongoing of the work.

IX. Recognition Council

The final step is to set a date for a Recognition Council. Here you invite sister churches to send messengers with their pastor to examine your statement of faith and organization. In Appendix 5 you will find a sample letter of invitation and a suggested order of service.

It is wise to have a resolution drawn up ahead of time, that the church will affiliate with the national association of churches — provided that there is favorable action on the part of the Recognition Council with respect to the new church.

X. Recording of Offerings and Registration Number

Financial stewardship is important from the opening day. You will naturally encourage believers to bring their tithes and offerings. In fact, if you know of several families who are planning to found a church with you, encourage them to start laying aside their offerings weeks before you start the work.

Many church planters order offering boxes for the opening day. It is easier for your financial secretary to keep a record of givings if people give through a numbered envelope.

In Canada you will need to apply for a registration number in order to give acceptable tax-deductible receipts. Have your clerk send the following information to your national denominational office, or, if your church is going to remain unaffiliated, send the information to the Department of Revenue and Taxation,

Church name and mailing address,
Pastor's name and mailing address,
Clerk's name, mailing address and occupation,
Treasurer's name, mailing address and occupation,
Names, addresses and occupations of trustees, if any,
Names, addresses and occupations of deacons,
Brief financial statement detailing income and expenditures, assets and liabilities,
Date the first service was held,
End of church fiscal year,
Church affiliating with a national group will add the following: A certified statement, typed on a separate sheet and signed by the church clerk and one other officer, that the church will "abide by the governing documents of the supervising body".

Notice the following suggested outline for churches affiliating with the Fellowship of Evangelical Baptist Churches in Canada:

At a meeting of the _____ Baptist Church held on
_____ the following motion was
passed: "That we accept the statement of faith of the
Fellowship of Evangelical Baptist Churches in Canada and
that we are in agreement with the bylaws of that body, and
hereby apply for affiliation".

                                    Certified by_____
                                              Church Clerk

                                    _____
                                              Office held

In the United States many new churches seek incorporation.
The details differ from state to state. Legal counsel should be
sought. The lawyer will submit your papers of incorporation to
the secretary of state. Then you may apply to your district
director of internal revenue for tax-exempt status.

XI. The Place of Prayer

From the opening day lead your people to pray. Prayer is one
of the distinctive responsibilities of a fundamental church. The
prayer service dates back to the early New Testament Church. It
is recorded of the first church in Acts 2:42 that prayer was a vital
part in the fellowship. In Acts 4:13 Peter and John after being in
the presence of God had such a countenance that the people
"Marvelled; and they took knowledge of them, that they had
been with Jesus". In Acts 12:5-17 there is the account of the early
church praying for Peter's release from prison. In Acts 13 the
early church prayed as Barnabas and Paul were commissioned
for their missionary work.

Teach believers how to pray and not simply say prayers. It is
recorded in Acts 9:11 that Ananias would find Saul praying. This
was a new experience for Saul. Up to that time he had been
accustomed to saying prayers as a Pharisee. In fact the Pharisees
were known for saying prayers in public to be seen of men. Paul
as a faithful Pharisee would have said many prayers. Now for this
first time it is recorded that he prayed. He saw the difference
between saying prayers and praying.

Make much of the prayer service. Vary the methods of prayer groups. Make definite needs known for prayer. Share answers to prayer. Have time for testimonies. Seek the face of God in praise and prayer.

XII. Things that Retard Church Growth

There are several things that can hinder church growth. One is holding too many business and committee meetings. You can save a lot of dissension by having fewer such meetings. Keep your people well informed, but bring only major items before the congregation for church action.

A second problem is "talking to yourself". This is what you are doing when you visit your own members frequently. It is easy to carry on internal communication. It is enjoyable to visit your people because you know a welcome awaits you. However, while you are spending time socializing with your own people, others in the community are dying without Jesus Christ. There is a secondary problem as well. As your work grows, you will have fewer opportunities to visit your founding families. This could cause a reaction on their part because you "spoiled" them in the early stages of church development. Granted, this would demonstrate immaturity on their part, but it can be avoided by concentrating your efforts to the non-Christian community.

Holding too many meetings can also hinder growth. You do not need to have a full range of church organizations and activities such as historic "First Church". This is the time to plan services that will contribute to the growth of the church. Most churches have a heavy schedule, but let us remember that an extravagant or unrealistic range of church organizations and activities may overtax the church's willing workers. When this is the case, the programme of the local church disrupts the Christian home instead of contributing to its formation and influence in the community. God founded three institutions: the family, the church and the state. The church needs to reinforce family life — not disrupt it with too many activities.

Another problem is overfeeding your sheep. You must spend time preparing messages, but this must be balanced with your outreach ministry. Those who feed on the Word should share the responsibility of reaching the lost community. Pendley Taylor says this:

> *Sometimes there is too much 'note taking' and not enough 'feet taking'. It would be well for the church to remember*

*that new Christians are much like plants. When they receive
too much water they will die as quickly as those who do not
receive enough. We need to heed the admonition of Jesus
regarding the fig tree that produced no fruit; that is, water,
prune and fertilize it, give it one more year and then if it
bears no fruit, cut it down (105:91).*

Be careful to avoid a clannish feeling on the part of members.
Cliques and small groups can hinder church growth. Watch for
peculiar features that might hold back development. A social
status, upper or lower, when in control or when one becomes
dominant, will deter progress. The same applies to race and
language. You will see growth in the dominant group but other
segments will not develop.

Perhaps the greatest caution to heed has to do with those you
receive into membership. The strength of your church is not its
building or its location, but its people. The other things have
their place, but only your members can carry out the real work of
the church. The initial method used for receiving members will
serve as a pattern for years to come. Be sure they are born-again.
Be sure they are in accord with what you are seeking to do. Be
sure they concur with the church's doctrinal statement. Melvin
Hodges gives good counsel:

*Also in his anxiety to enlarge the membership roll, or to get
financial or moral backing for his church project, the
worker should be careful about receiving those who profess
to be Christians but may come to him from other groups
with doctrines contrary to those which he preaches....
Another point where care should be excercised is with
groups that have split off from another congregation and
desire to affiliate with the new church. Sometimes these are
contentious people who have left their original congregation
because they could not have their own way. Such members
will likely cause problems later on, and their presence may
be more damaging than beneficial to the new church. The
number of members is not as important as their loyalty and
stability (35:51).*

Many pastors have had the joy of founding a church. There are
few pastors like Fred Vaughan, who have had the joy of founding
three churches. He rightly deserves the title, "Mr. Home
Missions".

Fred Vaughan graduated from Toronto Baptist Seminary, in
the 1948 class. That same year he began Newtonbrook Baptist
Church in Willowdale, Ontario, with 2 or 3 families. Twelve
years later he had a congregation of over 200.

In 1960 he moved his family to Rexdale, Ontario, and started Thistletown Baptist Church with about 4 families. Upon his resignation in 1972 he had a congregation with an average attendance of 220. This church started with the purchase of a school portable. Within five years the congregation had erected a beautiful, spacious, colonial-style building.

His third church was the Parkview Baptist, Halifax, Nova Scotia. Here with 2 families, he commenced services in the Seventh Day Adventist Church building. A year later services were moved to a new suburban area. In his third year of service a fine edifice was erected on a choice site between two developing communities.

Drawing from his experience of founding three churches, Pastor Vaughan suggests that you should pray much for the leading and guidance of God. In each field, he took a survey to find the area of greatest need. This was followed by the selection of a meeting place. Once this has been done, according to Pastor Vaughan, you are ready to get to work. Cultivate prayer support and promote services by means of advertising and visitation.

Fred Vaughan recommends a simple constitution and bylaws for new churches to serve as a guideline for new people who are unfamiliar with church government. He thinks it is best for the pastor to be the chairman of the deacons, simply because he is closer than anyone else to all aspects of the work and he is overseer of the flock.

According to Pastor Vaughan, in the early days of a new church you may have to use some non-members in various capacities such as ushers and even Sunday School teachers. This should not be allowed to continue indefinitely, however, as the work may be weakened. Other church planters feel they would rather build up the work using only those who have indicated their support through membership. This latter method may be slower. Each pastor must use his own judgment and follow his own convictions. At the same time, we must avoid using expediency for the sake of getting short turn gains.

Door-to-door visitation and following up references from other Christians provided Fred Vaughan with his main prospects. In the early stages he had a radio program. An advertisement was run weekly on the church page.

Mrs. Vaughan also made a major contribution to the ministry of her husband. A gifted musician, she would play the piano or organ, sing with her husband at the services, visit the ladies of the congregation, provide hospitality in her home and go out of her way to greet newcomers to the services.

Today, Newtonbrook, Thistletown, and Parkview Baptist Churches are thanking God for Pastor Fred Vaughan and his vision for needy areas. Let us pray that God will raise up more men who will see the vision, and like Fred Vaughan, establish New Testament churches.

Chapter 7

PLAN YOUR WORK, WORK YOUR PLAN

$\mathbf{Y}$ou have heard the saying, "Plan your work, work your plan". Those who carry this out can testify to the value of having a systematic plan of action. In starting a new church the pastor's personal schedule is important. He needs to plan specific goals. In addition he needs to work out a schedule for the church including short and long term goals.

I. Your Personal Schedule

Your personal schedule involves the priceless item of time. In Psalm 90 Moses seeks the face of God and in verse 12 prays: "So teach us to number our days, that we may apply our hearts unto wisdom". He recognizes that his time was limited. His desire was to include in his lifetime the best use of his days to the glory of God. Thus Moses set up priorities. This is essential in church planting.

There are many things you would like to do. For example, there are people to visit, books to read, things to do with and for your family, and many more projects that you could not, realistically speaking, hope to accomplish. When the former Prime Minister of Canada, the Honourable John Diefenbaker, while interviewed on television after the death of his wife, Olive, was asked, "What are your plans now?" He replied, "I don't have time enough to do all the things I would like to do". This is the problem many face. Planning your schedule will help establish priorities.

Now it is not easy for church planters to stop and plan the use of their time. By nature they are usually agressive. Action is part of their makeup. It is hard to sit down to carefully think ahead and work out a satisfactory schedule. Yet this is a wise policy. Dr. R. Alec Mackenzie tells of a college president who participated in a Management Institute. Following the sessions the president said, "Perhaps one of the most significant concepts I gained is that it is not a sin or a poor use of time for an administrator to sit, think, and plan rather than be an activist. That one concept has transformed my whole outlook (46:11)".

Many find through experience that time spent in planning will give meaningful results. A number of secondary matters will be left aside. More time will be assigned to the important things. Your mind will be working ahead and preparing you for those things that follow. You will experience a psychological uplift when certain projects are completed. In addition, you will actually carry out your activities with greater efficiency.

As a church planter, you need a schedule; otherwise you will be working twenty-four hours a day, seven days a week. There are many things to do in starting a new work. You have a limited number of workers. You have a small budget. You are anxious to get things done. This can result in an over-worked pastor. Before long, the law of diminishing returns sets in. How much better to plan your work schedule with a reasonable amount of time for all necessary activities. Dr. R. Alec MacKenzie claims that "Executives who consistently devote more than 45 to 55 hours a week to their jobs are in serious danger of impairing their efficiency (46:10)". The average church planter will spend from 55 to 65 hours a week in his work.

The first step in planning your schedule is to take an inventory of what you are now doing with your time. Several time saving specialist have advocated a careful log-taking of time for a period of two or three weeks. Take an 8½" x 11" sheet of paper and divide it into seven columns. Next, by drawing lines from top to bottom, divide it into eighteen equal spaces. You may then mark the time from 6 a.m. through to 12 midnight. You have now marked out boxes for eighteen hours a day for one full week. Now, keep a record of your activities. Use your own abreviations such as "L" for letter writing, "PH" for phone call and "I" for interview. You will discover what non-essentials occupy your time. You will be surprised at the amount of time you have been wasting. Leslie Flynn tells of an experience of Dr. Walter Wilson.

Years ago Dr. Wilson took three sheets of letter-size paper, ruled each one for fifteen minute periods from 6 a.m. to 11:00 p.m., then for three days jotted down what he did during each fifteen minute period. Then he applied three rules to each quarter segment: (1) Did this glorify God? (2) Did this bring a blessing to others? (3) Did this prove profitable to me? Dr. Wilson summerized his feelings:

I scratched off the time if it did not fit these tests. When I finished, 55 per cent of my time — over half — did not measure up. At the time I was operating a tent factory with two hundred employees, pastoring Central Bible Church with two hundred members, broadcasting daily at 7:00 a.m., and raising a family of eight children. When I saw this record, I completely changed my way of living and found I could do three men's work and not be a bit more tired. This inventory altered the course of my life (21:38).

II. Your Personal Goals

Your personal goals for the progress of the work need to be planned. Goal-setting will show where you are going and how you propose to get there. There are several steps to follow in drawing up goals. Perhaps the most important of these steps is to record your goals in writing. This communicates what you have in mind. This should be done in clear readable language. Ralph Gibbs shows the importance of writing:

In having written goals we find that they add a sense of value to the things that we are directing our attention to. They help us to concentrate so that we can think of more and more possibilities of how we can reach that goal. They help is to create a sense of purpose and even an anticipation of life as we think about the goal that we have set for ourselves or for our organization. They help us make good decisions because we find that it is easier to decide upon a course of action if we know exactly what it is that we are trying to accomplish. Written goals save time. This is particularly true when we realize that if we have a clear sense of our goals we are less likely to become pre-occupied with irrelevant activities. Written goals are great confidence builders; we know where we want to go and how we plan to get there. Written goals reduce conflict (99:2,3).

Be specific in your goal setting. Notice how these two goals differ: (1) Our Sunday School attendance goal will exceed that of last year. (2) Our Sunday School attendance goal will exceed that of last year by 25. Think through the implications of the above. It is one thing to state a goal in general terms but it is another thing to be specific.

Following through with your plans, you will want to consider how each goal will be achieved. Are there obstacles in the way? Are there certain things available to help you reach your goal? Here you seek to overcome obstacles and to make use of all available resources.

Establishing a time schedule for completion as well as check points will be of help in the successful attainment of your goals. Let's say that you want to see your Sunday attendance grow from 25 to 45 in four months. This means you will seek to have a net increase of five a month. You have simply taken your goal and broken it down into attainable steps. Thus, if you lag behind in one period you can redouble your efforts for the next period.

In establishing goals, it is important to plan with your people. A congregation willing to plan and establish goals is alive. People are encouraged when they sense they are part of a growing church, when they have had a part in goal-setting.

In a new work, you will want to plan toward the organization of the church, which will lead in turn to the calling of a recognition council. This implies the election of certain officials, who will also be part of the charter membership of the church. During this early period, you will also want to draw up a statement of faith and certain by-laws or a constitution, taking into consideration the confession of faith of your association of churches. (Note, your church's willingness to conform with the principles and practices and confession of faith of the association will greatly affect the decision of the recognition council.)

You will want to add various organizations to your church. Which one should be added first and when? What do you need before you establish a youth group or a weeknight activity for boys?

Your visitation work will require planning. Since many pastors fail to allow enough time in their schedule for visitation, this is not carried out effectively in their churches. Frank Bettger shared his personal experience of failure in the insurance business. One day, having returned to his office to pick up a few things, found himself listening to Mr. Walter LeMar Talbot, President of Fedelity Mutual Life Insurance Company. This is what he heard:

> *Gentlemen, after all, this business of selling narrows down to one thing — just one thing — seeing the people! Show me any man of ordinary ability who will go out and earnestly tell*

his story to four or five people every day and I will show you
a man who just can't help making good (8:13)!

Frank Battger said that this made a profound impression in his
life. His resolve was strengthened and renewed, from then on he
never looked back.

Your discipleship programme needs to be planned. Many of
the churches in the Fellowship of Evangelical Baptist Churches
in Canada use the SHARE manual. It is sponsored by the
Church Ministries Board. Rev. Alex Shook of Saanich Baptist
Church, Victoria, British Columbia, introduced SHARE with the
specific purpose of discipling church members. To provide the
time due consideration must be given in the planning of your
schedule.

III. Your Order of Services

Your regular services should be thoroughly planned. Many
churches get into a rut. Services, at times, are held in order to
maintain an image. Sometimes there is little planning for the
content. At times the leader will pick hymns a minute or two
before the service starts. Special music is often chosen five
minutes before the hour of commencement. You perhaps have
been at a service where someone is even called upon to sing
during the service, without any time for preparation. When
services are poorly planned, it is no wonder people stay home!

A music committee, responsible for the selection of special
numbers can help in this area. Sermon themes can be passed on
to the committee if you desire the hymns to be chosen by others.

IV. Your Number of Services

What about the number of services you are going to schedule?
There are those churches that feel you gage spirituality according
to the number of times you open the door for services. Have you
ever heard a church leader say: "Let's burn the lights every
night! It is possible to have your people so busy running to
services that they have little time to run to their neighbours with
the gospel. In starting a new work you have the opportunity to
establish a schedule that will best fit your ministry. It is not
something that you must fit into, but rather, one that you can
shape and direct according to your plans.

In order to conserve nights for visitation and family activities,
many new churches hold board meetings on the night of one of
their regular services. Family night, when prayer meeting and
youth activities are combined, has become a popular institution.

Plan your special activities well in advance. For example, there
are certain fixed dates that are observed each year, such as
Christmas, Easter, Anniversary Sunday etc. These days can be
planned several years ahead. This type of planning on the part of
pastors and leaders assures the congregation that you know
where you are going and how you plan to get there.

V. Your Board and Church Business Meetings

At times, pastors fail to plan well for board or church business
meetings. Business sessions can be crucial services. One never
knows what project is going to be paid. It is wise, in planning for
such sessions, to think through all possible reactions on the part
of members. Keep your board or church business meeting to a
proper schedule. Not a few pastors have memories of board
meetings lasting until midnight! This represents poor leadership.
Little value is accomplished after 10 p.m. Your men have worked
hard all day. They are tired. It is easy for things to get-of-hand.
In a new work there are many things to be handled in business
sessions; but it is better to let a small group deal with most
business items, leaving only the major considerations for the
congregation.

Many pastors take a short rest in the afternoon preceding a
business meeting. This is an aid for self-control and an even
disposition. Pastors have tempers too and can say things that are
best left unspoken.

Donald J. McNair offers good counsel on preparing for
business sessions.

> *The practice of prethinking the possible events that might
> occur in any given circumstance is extremely important in
> preparing for congregational meetings and church officer
> meetings. Any such meeting carries with it the possibility of
> an unexpected comment triggering a chain reaction of
> comments that, in only a few minutes, can change the entire
> direction of the work or even destroy it. Many times the
> thrust of these unexpected comments would have been
> considered in a thorough prethinking session. Then the
> chairman of the meeting would not be caught with his guard
> down; he would already have thought at least of
> rudimentary answers and would thus have kept the control
> of the meeting in his own hands (48:72).*

Church planters serving under the Home Mission Board of the
Fellowship of Evangelical Baptist Churches in Canada are
requested to submit an annual proposal of plans and objectives.
(See 1 in Appendix) Throughout the year these are checked by

the secretary to see where reinforcement and encouragement are required.

Example of a Church Planter Planner

Church planter Don Robins credits part of his success to planning. Don was enjoying a fruitful ministry with Pastor Robert Dunlop at Parkside Baptist Church, Moncton, New Brunswick. They were serving one of the largest Baptist Churches in what is known as "The Bible Belt of the Atlantic Provinces". God had been speaking to Don about pioneering. My phone call simply confirmed in his heart the knowledge that he should give serious consideration as to when and where God would have him minister. We met at the post office at Amherst, Nova Scotia, with his wife Janice and two other church planters, Fred Vaighan of Halifax and Clair Hofstetter of Dartmouth. It was clear from the initial session that Don was a church planter.

He moved to Lower Sackville, Nova Scotia, in November, 1975. For two months he planned and studied the field. Starting with one family, he knew God was going to build a fundamental Bible-believing church in that community. Services were started on January 11, 1976. In less than a year the Acadia Hall was filled to capacity.

Don seeks to plan his entire church programme from a few months to a year in advance. And yet, he tries to be flexible enough to take advantage of opportunities that appear during the year.

After basic meetings have been planned, he sets them aside to be completed at various times throughout the year. Usually the detailed plans are ready between three and four months ahead of schedule. This allows two full months for promotion in detailed form. Under ordinary circumstances the congregation hears about the upcoming meeting for the first time when the speaker and meeting dates have been confirmed. In this way the church can begin to pray for the meetings.

An example of planning is seen from the fact that as far back as September, 1975, months before the services got underway, he had already secured Pastor Robert Dunlop as guest speaker for the first anniversary services. Likewise, anniversary services were planned in January 1977 for 1978 and those for 1979 were arranged later in 1977. Don also does this type of planning for special annual evangelistic services and rallies, family life conferences and a Christian Home week. He makes much of Patriotic Sunday in July. Their television program, "God's

Wonderful People" was planned a year before the first program was aired.

Don carries out the same thorough planning for his messages. Four things are included in planning his messages. The first has to do with time available for preparation followed by the needs of the congregation. He seeks to maintain a balance in his messages from Bible teaching to services with an evangelistic thrust. Lastly, he seeks to have a fresh approach at all times.

His messages are usually planned for months ahead. This means that he knows the topic, has done the preparation, and knows the date on which each message will be delivered. Sometimes he knows the topic and the approximate date of delivery but schedules time for detailed preparation at a later date. For example, when he preached from the Book of Phillippians, he had the entire series ready and completed in note form before the first message was delivered.

He methodically plans his messages for three months in advance. He allows room for changes, to meet specific needs or to fit in special occasions that may arise.

In sermon preparation he has made it a practice to establish two files. In the first he keeps all sermon ideas that come to mind. In the other he has notes which come to mind suitable for a particular sermon topic. This material is gleaned from devotional or study times, from reading books and from messages other pastors have preached. The second file, furnishes him with material which can be readily completed.

Don uses a "priority pad" for daily use in planning his schedule. He adopted this method from a taped seminar by Dr. Tom Wallace, pastor of Beth Haven Baptist Church, Louisville, Kentucky. The first thing he does each morning is to take his pad and list everything that needs to be done that day. Next, he puts them in order of priority and then does them in that order. Whatever he doesn't get done probably didn't need to be done that day! This method enables him to give prime time to priority activities. (See II on Appendix for sample of priority pad.)

Long-range planning is a vital part of his ministry. He is flexible, however, and is willing to change his plans when circumstances require that he do so. To him, this type of planning gives direction to the total ministry of the church. He has set up certain objectives for the next 10 to 15 years. His goal is to have an attendance of 1,000 by about 1990. His long-range plans include the establishment of a residence for senior citizens, a Christian day school and a Bible Institute.

Pastors who plan well can echo the four-fold value of planning

that Leon S. Hill mentions: "Planning saves time and effort —
Planning saves confusion — Planning saves duplication — Good
planning makes a greater impact (81:).

In the final analysis, a leader plans for the future. Robert
Schuller has said it well:

> *Leadership is the key to church growth. If the church is to
> really succeed in its mission of witnessing effectively to the
> non-church world in the Twenty-First Century, we must
> develop dynamic, aggressive and inspiring leaders.*
>
> *And what is leadership? Leadership is thinking ahead,
> planning for the future, exhausting all possibilities, en-
> visioning problems and dreaming up solutions to them, and
> then communicating the possibilities and the problem-
> solving ideas to the decision makers. This is leadership.*
>
> *In any institution, the leader is the man who is thinking
> ahead of everyone else. He is not living in the past but in the
> future, for leadership draws its inspiration from future
> projections and not from past accomplishments. The leader
> is alert to movements, trends and evolving developments. He
> is literally thinking longer thoughts than anyone else is —
> and expressing them effectively (68:48)!*

Temple Baptist Church
Sarnia, Ontario

PREACH IT, BROTHER

Biblical preaching is the order of the day for the establishment of a local church. All else will not get the job done. Elmer Towns has well said that: "The preaching of the Word of God is still the greatest enticement to get people into the house of God (72:129)."

Alfred Fevez, a beloved French Canadian, led me to the Lord. Several months later we were talking about the large crowds a certain pastor had in his Sunday evening services. In fact, he was turning people away, as the auditorium would not hold the large attendances. He used films and music extensively, and was himself a professional chalk artist. For teenagers, it was the most enjoyable place to go on Sunday evenings. Mr. Fevez heard my praise for such entertaining evening services. In response he simply quoted: "Faith cometh by hearing, and hearing by the Word of God (Rom. 1.17)". It was not so much what the pastor did, but what he did not do. It was only a matter of time until that pastor gave up the ministry and turned to other fields. We can use films and other methods in order to reach souls, but not at the expense of preaching the Word of God.

A while back, a young graduate of a seminary asked a denominational leader for a list of musicians he could use in his new church. He went on to state that by using musical teams he hoped to build up a large attendance. The leader gave a wise

reply: "But what happens when the music stops?" We must heed
the exhortation of Paul in 2 Tim. 4:1,2 to preach the Word.
What does it mean to preach the Word?

I. Preach the Work and Ministry of Jesus Christ

This is what Paul did according to 1 Cor. 15:3,4. Jesus Christ is
the Good News we proclaim. Paul said: "We preach not ourselves, but Christ Jesus our Lord (2 Cor. 4:5)". Dr. Jack Scott,
President of Central Baptist Seminary, Toronto, suggests that:
"We are to preach in two ways. First, there is the KERYGMA,
the unabashed clear facts of Christianity. The facts of the birth,
life, death and bodily resurrection of Jesus Christ. Then there is
what is called DIDACHE. This involves explaining the meaning
and significance of these great facts upon which our faith is
based (85)."

After all that is said and done, this is the only type of
preaching that saves and satisfies. This was the thought expressed by Dr. Theodore Cuyler of the Lafayette Avenue Church
in Brooklyn, a great preacher and an effective servant of Jesus
Christ. He had served his church for thirty years and in his
closing sermon he spoke on the joys of the Christian ministry:

> *Today I write the last page in the record of thirty bright,*
> *happy Heaven blessed years among you... When my*
> *closing eyes shall look on that record for the last time, I*
> *hope to discover there only one name, the name that is*
> *above every name, the name of Him whose glory crowns this*
> *Easter morn with radiant splendor, the name of Jesus Christ*
> *(103).*

II. Preach the Word with Faith

It was Isaiah who quoted the Word of God: "My Word shall
not return unto me void (Is. 55:11)". It gives confidence to know
that God will honour the word that is faithfully presented. We do
not always know the people in our new church, especially
strangers who respond to our promotion, but we do know that
God has given us a message for them. It is reassuring to sense the
presence of the Holy Spirit knowing He is able to use the Word
and to quicken hearts and souls.

III. Preach the Word in an Orderly Fashion

Most church planters find it is a help to plan their messages
well ahead. Dr. William Fitch, formerly pastor of Knox Presby-

terian Church, Toronto, had the habit of living with a sermon six months before preaching it. Dr. Henry Serenson, pastor of First Baptist Church, St. Cloud, Minnesota, had his messages completed two weeks before delivery. He was never rushed for last minute preparation. There are a number of helpful books dealing with sermon preparation. Church planters would do well to read one a year.

IV. Preach the Word to meet the Needs of People

As you visit homes, hospitals and do counselling you will soon become aware of set needs. Many are sick. Some are depressed. A few are neurotic. All the people you meet have needs. One pulpit master has well said: "There's a broken heart in every pew".

"Billy Graham often describes his style as preaching with the Bible in one hand and the daily newspaper in the other. Truth and needs are the duet of sound pastoral preaching (17:35)."

Elmer Towns relates the ministry of James Singleton of the Tri-City Baptist Church of Temple, Arizona:

Singleton indicated that a minister preaches differently in a new church than in an old congregation. Indicating in an old congregation he can get by on theatrics, dramatics or pulpiteering, he noted that the new congregation is built on meeting the needs of his people. Instead of topical sermons Singleton is known for his practical messages. A member noted: 'He reaches into issues where people live. I can apply almost every sermon he has preached. Singleton tries to combine biblical content and revival fire in every sermon giving both doctrine and evangelism (73:67).

V. Preach the Word with Conviction

It is the authorative Word of God. It's not yours but the voice of God. You need not apologize for it. Let what Paul said go with you in your preaching: "For the preaching of the cross is to them that perish foolishness; but unto us which are saved it is the power of God (1 Cor. 1:8)". Ernest Mosley said: "The gospel is proclaimed to unbelievers in the confidence that the Holy Spirit will use it to call them to repentance and faith. The objective of the proclamation experience should be kept clear (53:114)."

This type of preaching leads one to preach for a decision. Dr. Nixon Burns, who for many years taught Homiletics at Toronto Bible College, reminded his students that every sermon should lead to a decision. The decision might be for salvation, separation from sin, tithing or some other issue dealing with life.

We can say with Paul: "Woe is me if I preach not (1 Cor. 9:16)". Thousands of ministers are going to face judgment before God for not having preached the Word.

VI. Preach a Positive Message

There are those who attack certain forms of dress, hair style and a host of other things. There is a place for negative preaching. Certainly the Ten Commandments are negative. But it can be overdone. It is interesting to note that negative preaching tends to draw negative people. Melvin Hodges gives a thoughtful word:

> *The planter of churches will avoid too great an emphasis on negative preaching in his message. However, some negative preaching is necessary. The sinner must hear the thunderings of God's righteous law against his sin in order to be awakened to his need of a Saviour. Idolatrous practices must be challenged in the name of the true God. Through the power of the Holy Spirit, the tragedy of a sinful life must be revealed, but all of this is only preliminary to pointing to the one true Saviour.*
>
> *Let is be careful not to give the impression that being a Christian consists in not doing certain things. The fact that a person does not drink, smoke, dance, or gamble does not make him a Christian, nor do the clothes, jewelry, or makeup that he or she does or does not wear (35:21).*

VII. Preach Personally to Yourself

We who preach do not always live according to what we proclaim. Even the greatest preacher must acknowledge in the presence of Christ: "We are unprofitable servants (Luke 17:10)". It is important that we remember our own personal needs and let the Word of God work in our hearts. Thus, when we preach tithing, we tithe ourselves. "We can trust each other," says Dr. Sam Howie of Iak Ridge, Tennessee. "Pastoral preaching is personal and credible. The chief role of the minister in the pulpit is to demonstrate the kind of person he is so that people will know whether they can talk to him about personal problems. It 'rings true'. It risks showing the character of the preacher (35:21)."

VIII. Preach Various Series of Messages

Most books on Homiletics will give insight as to variety.

This method of sermon preparation will save you time. It will also give your people direction as to where you are going. Best of all, it disciplines you to keep at your books.

IX. Preach Doctrine

In starting a new church you will likely have members from several different denominational backgrounds. This is all the more reason you need to teach the doctrines of our faith. As you indoctrinate your people they will be able to give an answer to those who ask of the hope that is within their hearts. Furthermore, they will also be able to deal with those who follow false cults.

In doctrinal preaching, you need to emphasize the distinctives of the evangelicals. Is the virgin birth of Christ important? What about the bodily resurrection of our Lord? To the average church-goer a number of these teachings mean very little. However, people have died for the Word rather than deny it. "Preach it, brother" and God will use you.

X. Preach after Thorough Preparation

You will fail in your church planting unless you give people food for their souls. It is possible to spend your time in many worthwhile activities, such as visitation work, at the expense of your study. It is not one or the other. It is a matter of balance. It was Hollis Green who said: "There is little reason for the church to congregate unless there is a strong pulpit personality with a distinctive message to challenge and inspire them to return (31:55)." Dare to ask yourself: "Am I satisfied with the message to be presented?" Hollis Green likens the work of the ministry in preparation to that of a surgeon or school teacher. He asked: "What would happen to the surgeon who entered the operating room unprepared? What action would take place if the school teacher or college professor were to neglect the necessary preparation? How long can preachers get by with less than adequate preparation for the pulpit (31:57)?"

XI. Preach it with Clarity

You want your sermon to have life as well as being applied to a life. You have gathered your material. You have a message to share. Now you need to look at the form in which it is presented. It is somewhat like a housewife who has baked a pie. She has most of the ingredients — flour, salt, strawberries and the other things that go into a strawberry pie. However she ends up with a hard crust and a tasteless filling. She neglected to add sugar and care!

There are two important aspects to form; the words you choose and the illustrations employed. Choose words that communicate your message. This means to use words that people understand. It is surprising the number of people in a public service who do not know the meaning of the biblical term justification. Either we use another word or explain the meaning of the word used. An explanation need not be long. You need only say that justification is the act of God in which the believer in Jesus Christ is forgiven of his sin and made righteous in the sight of God.

Every preacher should have a copy of Roget's Thesaurus. It takes time to choose words and similes but it pays off. It is one thing to say that a Sunday School teacher must work hard. It is something else to say that a Sunday School teacher must work like a miner in a landslide! The former says one thing and the latter says the same but much more.

Take time to plan illustrations that let in light on the truth. Jesus Christ used short illustrations. In Matthew 5:13 he said to the believer, "Ye are the salt of the earth". This seven word statement is full of meaning and understanding. Jesus Christ used stories. In Luke 15 he cites the parable of the prodigal son. Make much use of biblical illustrations.

Writing or typing your message out is a worthy exercise. In this way you will actually visualize the words employed and the illustrations used. Furthermore, it is good discipline in that you tend to cover the major steps in sermon preparation. Another benefit is that you digest it better yourself.

Another step is to preach it in front of a mirror using a tape recorder. Sit down and listen to yourself. If your wife gets bored or falls asleep then you know there is further preparation needed! Finally, have your sermon taped during the actual presentation so as to hear yourself as your people did.

Example of a Church Planter
Who is a Master in the Pulpit

Dr. Hal MacBain is an excellent example of a church planter who is also a mighty preacher of the Word of God. Today, he heads up the Foreign Mission Board of the Fellowship of Evangelical Baptist Churches in Canada.

Temple Baptist Church, Sarnia, Ontario, was started by Hal MacBain back in the thirties. Eight charter members who were baptized believers signed their Statement of Faith. There were seven more who were baptized within a couple of months, who at the time of the signing of the charter, were interested but were not able to participate because they had not been baptized. Years later, when he resigned to accept a call to Forward Baptist Church, Toronto, he left behind one of the largest Baptist Churches in Canada.

The church started off with two months of tent meetings, held each night except Saturday, during July and August. Hal MacBain invited some outstanding preachers to come and minister. The little nucleus that gathered was a result of these meetings. There were many who would have liked him to start a gospel church or an undenominational church, but when he said it was to be a Baptist church many of these people withdrew from the fellowship. Looking back MacBain felt it was the only thing to do, that is, to establish their doctrinal position from the very first.

MacBain preached well-balanced messages with something for believers and a strong appeal for unbelievers in most messages. He believes that pastors must be persuasive even though it is not by human argument or eloquence that people are saved. It is important to present the gospel for a decision and the Holy Spirit seems to bless this kind of ministry.

He believes in preaching for a decision. This is one of the vital keys to reaching people for Christ. The message must be very clear. The issue must be presented forcefully. The challenge must be made or people will go away with a "so what" attitude.

He stated the following response to the question, "Do you give invitations?

Generally I gave an invitation both morning and evening, both at Temple Baptist Church, Sarnia, and Forward Baptist Church, Toronto. This does not mean that there were times when I did not give an invitation for people to come to talk about salvation, baptism, and church membership. It was generally a three-fold invitation and explained very carefully that coming forward was not the means of salvation but only a means of contact for us to be able to talk to people who were concerned enough to present themselves at the front of the church.

He offers the following suggestions for new church planters when it comes to preaching.

1. Get many books of sermons and read them. I have hundreds of sermons and have always appreciated reading the messages of great preachers.

2. Do preliminary study without the assistance of commentaries or other messages on the same subject. Work hard at gathering simple illustrations so that people will clearly un-

derstand what is involved. After you have done everything you can in preparing the messages on your own, then look up commentaries and other men's ministry on this subject and the results may or may not fill in some gaps that are still there.

3. Do practise preaching on your own in your own bedroom or some place where you are away from people. You should preach in front of the mirror, preach to the bedpost, and let your voice be audible. Get accustomed to using words while standing on your feet preferably when no one else is around.

Responding to the question as to the place of the pulpit in the field of church growth, MacBain said:

> *I am convinced that many devices and much methodology can go for naught if the people are not receiving something worthwhile when they come to the church. We can organize ourselves very well in methods of getting people into the church but if they do not get something worthwhile when they get there they are not going to come back and it is always going to be a problem to try to build up the ministry. I believe that the pulpit alone is not sufficient to attract people. It is necessary for us to use both the methods of getting people in and the preaching of the Word with power. It is important that we do not try to isolate one of these and say that this is the way that a church is built. Actually, it is by using all areas of ministry that churches are built.*

Let's keep in mind the counsel of Donald McNair: The ministry of preaching will always be a part of the life and work of the church (48:45)."

You will appreciate the testimony of Pastor Don Robins of the Temple Baptist Church, Lower Sackville, Nova Scotia, which he gave at the close of his first year of church planting: "As I continue to reflect upon the first year, I see three major keys to our growth. They are, much prayer, strong Bible preaching and a never-ending door to door evangelism (84:21)."

We are in full accord with the quotation used in the opening part of this chapter: "The preaching of the Word of God is still the greatest enticement to get people into the house of God (72:129)".

Chapter 9

REACH THE REACHABLE

Two tools necessary for an adequate outreach of a local church are a thriving Sunday School and a planned visitation ministry. They should be developed simultaneously, each reinforcing the other. As with other phases of ministry, there must be balance. A. R. Tippett suggests: "An indigenous church must grow as any other, in three dimensions — quantitatively, qualitatively, and organically. There should be a certain balance in the growth. If one outstrips the other, we get distortions of growth (7:126)."

One church planter went out and built up a large Sunday School, mainly made up of children. As a result, there was chaos. The few adults were worked to such an extent that a number left and went to other churches. It was not surprising that the new church did not continue but merged with another church. What was the problem? The church planter failed to reach heads of families. His reports showed excellent growth in numbers. As George Bell of Oakwood Baptist Church, Toronto, says: "It is easy to confuse statistical gains with real gains. Child and youth often bring quick numerical growth but not the leadership or finance for continued growth. Failure in putting a priority in reaching men, can hamper a new church."

Fuller Institute of Church Growth suggests that the average church receives more new members by biological growth or by transfer than by new converts unrelated to the church. Biological growth refers to children of parents who are members of the church. Transfer growth is a reference to people who move into the community from another church. This growth will not do for a new church. The reason for this is when there are too few people to begin with you do not have sufficient for biological growth. Furthermore, if you wait for new families to move into the community you will grow too slowly to become a self-supporting church. Thus the new church is forced to go out and find new converts to the glory of God.

It is sad to see some established churches become somewhat stagnant churches. An evangelical church should continue, even after many years of ministry, to reach new families. Evangelism is not a preliminary step in order to have a church, rather it is the fulfillment of the Great Commission. As such it should be the desire of every born again believer to share the Good News, and in doing so, enlarge his home church. We need to "Reach the reachable!" How?

I. The Sunday School is an Agency for Church Growth

"As goes Maine, so goes the nation", is an expression often heard during the American election returns. This may or may not be so. It is true however, "As goes the Sunday School, so goes the church". A growing Sunday School with a fine balance of children, youth and adults will produce a growing church.

There are a number of reasons why the Sunday School fosters church growth. The Sunday School appeals to all ages. It puts people to work. It provides a social setting for people to get together with others in their own age bracket with similar interests. It involves people in studying the Word of God. Pastor Gordon Phillips in addressing a group of church planters in British Columbia said: "I am particularly interested in the Sunday School because of its unquestioned status in many minds today. I believe in the Sunday School. It is only a vehicle but one of the very best vehicles we have of reaching the masses with the Word of God." He went on to add: "We need to strike out the notion that Sunday School is for children only and make the priority group with the priority organization of the Sunday School — ADULTS. Reaching adults in the study of God's Word is the key to reaching entire families for faith in Jesus Christ."

The staff and officers of the Sunday School should be baptized members of the church and serve only with the church's approval. The pastor sets an example for others as he carries on an active role in the Sunday School.

The teaching staff should be known by their punctuality, arriving at least fifteen minutes before Sunday School starts. In this way they can visit with newcomers and spend extra time with those who come early. They should have a good record for attendance.

The time has come to make the Sunday School a "school". Too much time is spent on "opening exercises" and announcements. The major portion of the hour should be in the Word. Avoid unnecessary disturbances.

Our public schools are well furnished. The Sunday School should have some basic tools in the line of audio-visual aids. A central picture library including flannel graph and filmstrips is helpful.

Curriculum planning is important. It is better to use one set of Sunday School materials throughout the school, than to mix several publishers, according to the individual desire of each teacher. You avoid this problem when a Christian Education Committee is appointed to oversee the Sunday School.

Many pastors use a covenant or set up standards for their teachers. Dr. Jack Hyles of First Baptist Church, Hammond, Indiana, has the following requirements:

1. Faithful attendance to all the public services of the church.
2. Strict adherence to the church's policy concerning separation from the world.
3. Giving the tithe as commanded in the Scriptures.
4. Loyalty to the entire program of the First Baptist Church.
5. Faithful attendance at the Sunday School.
6. Faithful attendance at the Wednesday evening teacher's meeting.
7. A regular weekly time of visitation on behalf of the Sunday School class. (37:94).

II. A Bus Ministry can assist in Church Growth

A bus ministry, if worked properly, can contribute to the growth of the Sunday School and church. Develop the ministry of bussing by setting as a goal the reaching of parents. This involves personal follow-up and soul-winning. Plan activities for the whole morning including a children's church or else have a part for children in the morning service. Avoid the mistake of many churches which provide a bus ministry for only the one hour Sunday School session. Keeping children the whole morning might reduce the total potential attendance but in the long run it will enhance the quality of the ministry. Go bussing and you will grow.

There is considerable merit in what the Southern Baptists call the Flake's Formula for Sunday School growth. It has five ideas:

1. Locate the prospects.
2. Enlarge the organization.
3. Enlist and train the workers.
4. Provide the space.
5. Go after the people (70:36).

Eugene Skelton in writing an introduction for Andy Anderson's book, "Where the Action Is" speculates:

> *I predict a fantastic future for your Sunday School! I predict more people enrolled in Bible study through Sunday Schools than we have ever dreamed of seeing. I predict the improvement of teaching in our Sunday Schools and the winning of vast numbers of people to Christ through the witness of Sunday School workers and class members. In saying this, I realize I am going counter to what many say, some of them Christian leaders and others religious educators. I still make my predictions (1:13).*

One Example of a Church Planter Who built a Sunday School and Through it a Great Church

Dr. E. Sidney Kerr majored in the Sunday School. He commenced his ministry in Preston, Ontario, in 1963 with about 85 in attendance. Upon his retirement in 1976 the Sunday School was averaging 600. His first year budget was $7,800 whereas in 1977 it was over $140,000. It could be said of Sid Kerr and the Temple Baptist Church that they could have had the motto: "More than the year before!"

He and his church leaders were constantly recruiting and training new people. In this way the church had an ongoing training ministry.

A multiple staff was another tool that assisted in the growth that came about over the years. He claims that one pastor can only handle a maximum of 200 to 250 people. This is where you add additional staff with talents than can supplement the senior pastor.

Adequate facilities are a necessity. During his ministry at Temple, the church had six successful building programs. In the planning of the additions, emphasis was placed upon large functional areas, and they were built according to the ministry planned for the area.

Visitation was a real part of the ministry. Week after week the members would average a minimum of 300 calls. The pastors likewise carried out an extensive visitation ministry. Pastor Kerr had the familiar motto: "Never ask your people to do something you are not doing". He claims that "Great churches are built through a solid, steady, regular visitation programme. Busses have been a key to our visitation programme. While advocating the wise us of busses, we do not recommend the indiscriminate use of such vehicles to bring in hundreds of children, for whom we do not have sufficient staff or proper facilities. This is especially true of pre-schoolers.

III. A Planned Visitation Ministry is a Necessity

This is a necessary ministry for a new church. Ron Smith gives the following background on visitation:

The word visitation comes from the same root as the word vision. It means to go and see someone, to extend friendship, comfort or help. Proverbs 29:18 tells us 'Where there is no vision the people perish'. Is it not equally true where there is no visitation the people perish? With regard to Christian visitation, the visitor should have as his primary objective the communication of the Good News of the Gospel. Merely to make friends is good but is not good enough. Some visitors stop short at the mere social call.

There are hundreds of scripture illustrations which teach us that visitation is the basic means of reaching people. In Genesis 3, we read of God who visited Adam and Eve in order to restore the fellowship that had been broken by sin. In Judges 6, the Lord visited Gideon to announce that he would be used to lead Israel against her enemy.... The Lord Jesus Christ visited as a major feature of His earthly ministry. Jesus Christ made a point of moving among people, visiting them along the seashore, in the highways at the gates of their cities and in their homes (71).

Many varied programs and activities can be carried on by the local church. They are good and worthwhile. However, it is possible for a new church to take on too many services and ministries. Some new churches are so loaded down with activities that visitation is secondary. These other ministries, especially in a new church, can be detrimental to its growth. This does not mean that there is anything wrong with other programs. It is a question of setting priorities. In starting a new church one must choose activities that will stimulate growth. Elmer Towns suggests this:

*House to house visitation will find mature Christians who
may be languishing in dead churches. Older Christians can
give money, teach classes and win souls. Rudy Holland
balances these contrasting opinions with the following
quotation: 'The visitation program will net those people who
have been made aware of your church as a result of advertising. Your church should have an active visitation
program. Teaching soul winning is a vital part of visitation.
Emphasize every visit primarily as a soul winning call and
only secondarily as a church prospect call (73:132).*

Church planters have brought about fine growth through door
to door visitation. Thorald Marsaw in his first monthly report
dated June 8, (1977 stated: "Praise God there were over 60 family
prospects through door to door visitation".

Visitation is one of the finest ways for pastors to build up a
prospect list, thus establishing a set program of homes to visit.
Dr. Jack Watt had a habit of visiting fields and asking pastors to
show him their prospect list. In his judgment every pastor should
have a minimum of 100 families on such a list.

Records are necessary for follow-up. Many pastors use 3 x 5
cards. Utilizing one card for the four sides of a block, the address
is noted. A code can be developed where Pr. — Presbyterian,
R.C. — Roman Catholic, NI — Not interested, P — Prospect. A
"P" should have a date next to it for follow up within a week or
two. Place this on your calendar.

IV. Problems Faced in getting Visitation Started.

One of the problems of visitation work like many other activities is getting started. The devil will do all in his power to keep
a new church from developing a visitation ministry. One way
Thorald Marsaw found helpful was to take out one or two of his
interested members. After several weeks they soon inspired
others to participate in the ministry. But it is interesting to note
that he started this at the commencement of his work. The time
to start visitation is now, this week.

Another problem is one of fear. This can we met by having two
go together. Perhaps at the start you and your wife. In many ways
it is better, in the day time when men are working, to have your
wife with you.

Many have not seen the value of visitation and so have neglected it. The Sunday bulletin of Fellowship Baptist Church,
Coburg, Ontario, had the following for October 30, 1977.

The Value of Visiting...

1. I visit because there are matters than can be settled or

started for human good and God's glory only by visit.

2. I visit because it is the only known method to build a Sunday School successfully.

3. I visit because it is the best known way of reaching absent absentees and winning them for regular attendance.

4. I visit because it is the best way of keeping in touch with my members.

5. I visit because my visits count more than telephone calls or letters.

6. Visitation creates in the mind of the visited: 'Somebody cares for me and is interested in me'.

7. Visitation creates a more responsible hearing on the part of the visited for teacher, class department and church. Many pupils have said: 'My teacher loves me, a visit proved it'.

8. Visitation builds spiritually both the visitor and the visited. There have been times when people have visited homes using wrong principles — such as negativism or ill-manners. This can result in frustration and defeat. There is no need to criticize what you see in the home.

Some overstay their visit and this too can be self-defeating. It has been the experience of some churches to visit the same family 4 to 6 times in one week. This happened because the visitation work was not planned.

Pastor Don Howard of Calvary Baptist Church, Ottawa, Ontario, in his article on Visitation has well said: "The placing of a welcome sign in front of our church building will not pack the auditorium. Sending a bus throughout the community will never fill the Bible School. No program, no matter how well organized, will ever take the place of a strong outreach visitation in the area of the local church (82:7)."

It is noteworthy that a church does not need a lot of people engaged in this ministry to see results. Ten couples averaging ten door to door calls a week will cover 5200 homes a year. God has prepared souls for your calls!

Abe Funk in his manual on visitation evangelism stresses the need to keep the program alive.

More than any other program of the church, visitation will need special attention to keep it functioning smoothly. Don't be satisfied just to have a program; keep it at its maximum!

1. Keep visitation before the people.
   a. Preach it regularly.
   b. Teach it in the Sunday School and other organizations.
   c. Announce it in each Sunday bulletin.

d. Make reports at each business meeting.

e. Secure films, film strips, outside speakers, qualified to speak on this subject, and expose the entire church to these.

f. Bring your area map to prayer meeting and pray for your field by area.

g. Have regular testimonies of good calling experiences.

2. Variety of calling — Give a calling team a variety of calls.

Have a team make two or three prospect calls, then for variety give them a fellowship call on one of the church members simply for the sake of fellowship. This may be an elderly couple or a sick member. Give them the change of calling area as well (23:4,5).

One Example of a Church Planter Who knew How to Visit and to get His People Visiting

Pastor J. Roger Fines was called to be a church planter in North Sydney, Nova Scotia, by the Fellowship Baptist Home Mission Board. Under his leadership the church was self-supporting within twenty-four months. He credits a consistent visitation ministry as a key to growth. He adopted Jerry Falwell's definition of saturation evangelism which is "Preaching the gospel by every available means to every available person, at every available time."

How did he apply saturation evangelism in North Sydney? He led his church in purchasing a good used offset press. They were thus able to print gospel tracts, including the name and address of the church, for distribution to the entire city. A fine door to door visitation with an emphasis on soul-winning was carried out. A bus ministry, and a monthly gospel paper, "The Gospel Light" became a meaningful part of the outreach ministry. His church would advertise weekly along with occasional television and radio advertisements.

His visitation ministry is planned to reach the community. He goes door to door soul winning every Thursday and Friday afternoons and often on Saturday morning while on bus visitation with the bus workers. The church has a regular visitation program every Wednesday. This is mainly a soul-winning and follow-up ministry. All Sunday School teachers and bus captains are responsible for the follow-up of their respective students and and they fill out a worker's card each week to report their week's activities. Each Sunday School teacher is given a follow-up card for every absentee in his/her class which is filled out and returned the next week to insure that every absentee is followed up, every week.

Although his emphasize is on soul-winning visitation, he seeks to be flexible rather than mechanical in his approach. He likes to work for a decision when possible. There are times when the Holy Spirit says 'no, another time,' so he does not press the matter. His aim is to get people saved, but God has to show the work and prepare the way.

Roger Fines suggests to church planters that they learn from men who have done the job. Read about them, talk to them, ask them questions, learn what they are doing and why! He thinks too many take the advice of a loser and turn out the same way! He would advise us to follow a winner! Learn from others. Remember, methods vary but principles remain the same.

People can be reached. The emphasis on a great Sunday School and a well-planned visitation ministry will help "Reach the reachable!"

Chapter 10

Riverside Baptist Church
Windsor, Ontario

DOLLARS AND SENSE

Dollars combined with common sense will make it possible for you to purchase the essentials. One needs to handle finances according to definite Bible principles.

I. All that We have is His

Principle number one is that all that we have is his. You have sung the verse written by William W. How. "We give Thee but Thine own, What e'er the gift may be; All that we have is Thine alone, A Trust, O Lord from Thee." Life takes on real meaning when we recognize that everything belongs to the King. Putting this principle to work means that God who is aware of our needs, will provide as we put our faith in Him.

In the early stages of your church draw up an inventory of needs. Establish priorities of things you can use before the edifice is erected and those things that will be required later. Such items should include basic office equipment. Printing is a necessity and so a scanner and an offset press are useful. The latter can be a used one and purchased for a reasonable price. Do not overlook visual aids such as a slide filmstrip projector, a cassette recorder and record player. More and more pastors are making use of an overhead projector in their teaching ministry. A polaroid camera is handy for historic shots of important events as well as for a review at the annual watchnight service.

Some pastors make this list of needs available to their church families. The list can also be included in your prayer letters to supporting churches. You will find many people who will willingly buy items for anniversaries and other special days.

II. A Definite Portion should be returned to the Lord

Principle number two is that a definite portion should be returned to the Lord. From Matthew 23:23 we come to the conclusion that our Lord did not do away with the tithe. Putting this principle to work means that there will be sufficient funds for the work if the people are led to give in a Biblical manner. In place of begging for funds we seek to motivate giving on behalf of Jesus Christ. This is what Paul did in Romans 12:1. Harold Longenecker has well said: "The problem is finally reduced to this issue: Our instructions in the realm of money must have as their chief concern the glory of God. Money must not be made the major object (44:75)."

You will need to set up a teaching pattern. Some pastors devote three to four full messages a year to the subject of stewardship of time, talent and treasury. A brief sentence can be given at the time of the offering. Short items can appear in the bulletin. Give new members boxes of envelopes upon their reception. This is in keeping with the counsel of Elmer Towns:

> Give every person an offering envelope. This encourages people to give because it provides a confidential means of giving. Tell every person to ask God what he would have them give. As a pastor point out that God knows the need. He knows every part that each of your people should have in the offering. If all are obedient to God they will be blessed and the need will be met (73:69).

You are doing the believers a favor by encouraging them to give. They will feel better and they will have a vital interest in the work.

III. We must give an Account of our Stewardship

Principle number three is that we must give account of our stewardship. First, we must give an account to God according to Romans 14:12. In addition we must, as leaders, give an account to our people. Accountability forces careful judgment as to how funds are used. Oftentimes funds are wasted on things that really do not advance the work of the local church. This is especially so in the erection of a building. There are many things that you would like to have in an edifice. This is not the issue. The question is, is such an item needed? Will it really help the growth of the church?

It must be added that one should not be "penny-wise" or "pound foolish". There are ways to reduce expenditure and things that can be eliminated. However, one should not short change on equipment at the expense of a more useful ministry. Dollars make sense when one plans carefully.

IV. Let the Lord's People know of the Local Needs

Principle number four is to let the Lord's people know of the local needs. In 2 Corinthians 8, Paul told the church about specific needs. Putting this to work means you will keep the church informed of the total financial picture. Have regular reports from the treasurer. Plan for the people to give in response to the need.

You notice in Phil. 4:15 that Paul commended the people for their support. This is a verse that may be used in leading the people to give. It is encouraging to hear a pastor thank the church on behalf of Jesus Christ.

V. The Pastor is Worthy of His Hire

Principle number five is that the pastor is worthy of his hire. In I Timothy 5:18 we read: "Thou shalt not muzzle the ox that treadeth out the corn. And the labourer is worthy of his reward." It is up to the pastor to teach the church this concept. Organize your board and church to examine annually your remuneration and travel expenses. The cost of living because of inflation must be kept in mind.

In setting up your annual budget, separate your travel allowance from your remuneration. Your travel should be reported as part of the upkeep of the work, not of your remuneration.

Too many buildings have been erected at the expense of the pastoral remuneration. Too many pastors suffer at the expense of heavy missionary offerings. Actually, the pastor is to blame in such cases because in a new work he can lead the way and set up proper steps for putting together a balanced budget. The pastor is the church's most valuable human asset. If this is so, his needs should be cared for by his people.

VI. Don't spend More than You take in

Giving leadership in the area of finances should be a part of your ministry. Elmer Towns tells about Pastor James Singleton of the Tri-City Baptist Church, Temple, Arizona:

> *Singleton tells young preachers, 'Next to my Bible I study my financial statement most'. He tries to make his people cost conscious because to him money is ministry. The way we handle our money is the way we handle our ministry. He lists some very simple rules for the young preacher starting out.*
>
> 1. Don't spend more than you take in.
> 2. Income should increase in proportion to membership.
> 3. Always know how much money you have in all accounts.
> 4. Keep good credit in your community. Pay all your bills or arrange for credit (72:69).

Over-spending is a serious problem for a new church. There are many needs, and finances are limited. You must choose carefully which items you purchase, following your priority sequence. Dr. Truman Dollar of the Kansas City Baptist Temple gives this caution:

> *Probably one of the most difficult and frustrating problems for the pastor of a growing and agressive church is to control budget expenditures within projected limits. Some of the problems are related to the very nature of a growing church, while others are directly attributable to imprudent and in temperate spending by undisciplined staff members (15:93)*

This leads to a consideration of indebtedness. A young church needs to understand what debt is and how to handle it. Dr. Robert Schuller suggests: "We borrow money for this church but we don't borrow money for coal. We borrow money for everything that has collateral, non-depreciable value, but we don't borrow money for our television ministry, for interest on the capital debt, for salaries or for utilities (67:27)."

Planning for a building calls for budgeting of the finances. Most new churches plan, construct and complete a building program within the first five years. Such a budget includes property, site development including landscaping and parking, and the cost of the edifice with furnishings and equipment. One should not overlook other payments such as legal, loan, and architectural fees. Your general budget must also allow for the increased maintenance of the new building.

Your maximum debt limit should not exceed four times your annual income. This annual income should not include grant support coming from other churches or any other special short-term income situations. For example, a church with an income of

$35,000 per annum might consider a loan in the range from $105,000 to $140,000.

There is a limit on the amount you can secure on a first mortgage through an institution. Generally this loan will be no greater than 75% of the lender's appraised value.

Interest rates must be taken into consideration. Jim Rawson who served as a member of the Fellowship Baptist Home Mission Board and who is a mortgage broker suggests: "Be aware of interest rate structure at the time of a loan application. Don't ask for unreasonable consideration. Most knowledgeable lenders are aware of the financial position of churches and will be as considerate as possible (96:2)." He adds the following:

Term and amortization period should be as long as possible. You need to understand the terms-amortization and term. By amortization you have in mind a period of time wherein a constant monthly payment to principal and interest will repay total amount of loan. A term is a period of time wherein terms of loan will remain constant. If the term is a shorter period than the amortization then at the conclusion of the term the loan is subject to principal repayment or the completion of a renewal agreement based on terms and conditions existing at the time of renewal.

The best combination is a term and amortization of equal duration.

Privilege clause — Most institutional lenders will permit the payment of a principal amount on an annual or semi-annual basis. The amount varies from 5% to 100% of the original loan depending on the policy of a given institution. This payment is of course without any interest penalty or bonus (104:2).

Many churches carry on a building program through the issuance of church bonds. Sometimes this is simply a promissory note. It is better to have it secured with a second mortgage as it means much more to the lender.

There are a number of advantages of using bonds. The loan amount could be as high as 100% of value if the bonds are fully sold. The interest rate is generally 1 to 2% lower than institutional mortgage rates. Many times people who receive the semi-annual or quarterly interest payments will return them to the church in the form of an offering. Likewise a number of bond holders eventually will turn their bonds in as offerings.

However, there are some real disadvantages. The church might run into a problem if a large number requested repayment. This is why you need a required 30 or 60 day waiting period before the bond can be redeemed. Bookkeeping, if handled internally, often creates a problem.

One of the ways to assist a church is through the type of program advanced by the Fellowship Baptist Home Mission Board. It is called the Church Adoption Plan. The objective is to assist new churches in the purchase of a land site and/or the erection of a new edifice. The plan is to encourage an established church to share its financial resources with a new church. This can be done by the donor church borrowing on its own property equity and giving the amount, in the form of a loan, to the new church. It is suggested that the donor church make this loan available interest-free for the first five years or, if this is not possible, at a reduced rate. Repayment of principal could be arranged so that the portion of the principal due in the early years of repayment could diminish with the amount increasing each year. It is further suggested that the donor church arrange with its own bank to be the serving and collection agency.

This plan has been a great help to a number of new churches. Erin Mills Baptist Church, Mississauga, Ontario, was greatly encouraged when High Park Baptist Church, Toronto, extended an interest-free loan of $25,000 and Long Branch Baptist Church, Toronto, $15,000. This same procedure enabled Northside Fellowship Baptist Church, Regina, Saskatchewan to move ahead with their building plans when Emmanuel Baptist Church, Chatham, Ontario advanced an interest-free loan of $25,000.

Actually this plan helps the new church face four problems that many times hinder their growth: the high price of land, the steep price of construction, limited financial resources and limited borrowing power.

It is obvious that a suitable site and a functional building provide four things to the new church: it tends to stabilize the church, it becomes a testimony to the community, it provides for a fuller ministry and it fosters growth which ultimately leads to a self-supporting church.

Allow enough time for the donor church to become acquainted with the new work. The pastor of the donor church can be invited to visit the field with his deacons if distance is not a factor. In this way the men go back and present what they have seen to the church with great zeal.

It should go without saying that your own personal budget must be a balanced one. It is of utmost importance that you make your own payments on time and according to your agreement. Paul might well have meant this or certainly implied, in writing to Timothy about pastors having a "good report of them which are without (I Tim. 3:7)". Pastors must live within their means. Harold Longenecker counsels:

Below are some questions the minister might ask himself as he considers ways of curtailing expenses:

1. Do I take a daily paper? Why? Is it essential?

2. To how many secular magazines am I subscribing?

3. Do I buy things that I do not need simply because they are 'on sale'?

4. Am I careful about the use of electricity?

5. If I heat my own home, do I use fuel judiciously?

6. Do I buy unnecessary food items in addition to the essential staples, or do I purchase more expensive commodities than required?

7. Do I buy the less expensive cuts of meat or the more choices pieces? (Some of the least expensive items on the meat stand are the most valuable to proper diet balance).

8. Have I tied myself down to the burdensome monthly payments for appliances, luxuries, or a late model auto? If so, can I sell one or more of these items and so alleviate the stress (44:100).

In the Appendix you will see the financial questionnaire used by the Fellowship Home Mission Board to give a better picture of the status of a prospective church planter. It is used only by the office and the information is confidential. It was developed due to a church planter who was appointed to a field, and two months later, faced a financial crisis. Before his appointment he had two loans with high monthly payments. The loans were for a long term. The financial problems started to affect his ministry. Further, the remuneration he was receiving would not enable him to meet his obligations. Had his situation been known ahead of time a different course would have been followed.

Example of a Church Planter Who Understands Finances

Pastor Alan Silvester is one leader who knows how to plan finances for a local church. He was called to Riverside Baptist Church in February, 1974. At the time the church had an indebtedness exceeding $325,000. Weekly offerings were running below $600. which was the amount needed to cover the interest on the debt. Many bond holders were calling for their money. One or two threatened court action. The church was being talked about in various Christian circles in the city. The members were downcast as to the future. The large debt and deficit financing virtually destroyed the morale of the people.

There were few alternatives. One would have been to declare bankruptcy. The problem with this course was a matter of paying off the debt. The actual value of the building and property would not be sufficient. A second factor would have been to appeal to a national fellowship, apply for affiliation and seek the necessary support. It was in response to this appeal that the Fellowship Baptist Home Mission Board made it possible for Alan Silvester to commence his work in April, 1974. It was really a miracle how God used him to lead the work in planned steps, from the depths of financial ruin to a strong solvent position today.

One of the first steps was to communicate with the bond holders. This was done on a personal basis with church members working hand-in-hand with the pastor. Assurance was given that the work was continuing. Each was asked to have patience and their bonds would be secured.

A second step was what Pastor Silvester calls "Operation Miracle" Sunday. He sensed the leading of the Lord to challenge the people to set aside a Sunday in June, 1974, for a really large offering. He presented it to the finance committee, the deacons and then to the church. It was received enthusiastically. The objective was arrived at through prayer, a consideration of the needs of the church and the ability to meet it. Faith had always been the primary ingredient in this undertaking. Now this is an annual event and has been well received by the church.

The following were the objectives and the amounts received:

Year	Objective	Offering
1974	$18,000	$14,000
1975	15,000	15,000
1976	18,000	18,000
1977	17,000	15,000

"Operation Miracle" Sunday is a great boost to the morale of the congregation. It is a spiritually health-giving activity. One of the newer members suggested it be carried on even after the present financial need is met.

The pastor operates with a church budget. Purchases are anticipated as much as possible and incorporated into the budget. Then the money is spent only if it is actually on hand. Special items such as choir gowns, movie projector and screen are purchased through an annual Christmas offering.

Al Silvester believes in good audio-visual equipment. The church has purchased two overhead projectors, a 16 mm movie projector, a film-strip projector, built in screens, good cassette recording equipment and a photocopier.

"Systematic giving is an outgrowth of a committed heart", says Alan Silvester. "When the heart is right the pocket book will be too. We don't say a lot about it. I do preach on it occasionally."

The example of the pastor leads the way. God has enabled Alan Silvester to give generously above and beyond the tithe. When the pastor leads the way he can challenge others to follow with conviction and authority. In the words of the pastor: "Faith, prayer, sacrificial giving and sound financial management have helped restore the church to health and strength again".

The same prescription will work for you.

Chapter 11

DON'T HIDE YOUR LIGHT

"**W**hen the saying was noised abroad, the multitudes came together." Samuel Farina suggests that this is a great text (Matt. 9:31) for church planters. "We like to see many come to our services. It can happen. Good promotion — publicity — advertising — all can help you achieve this goal (87:19)."

The way we promote will determine to a certain degree the type of congregation that will come together. There are ways to promote your new church that will draw a crowd — and that's about all you will have. One pastor said if he had a certain number in Sunday School he would stand on his head. In another situation the Sunday School superintendent had the privilege of throwing a cream pie in the face of his pastor because their attendance goal was met. These methods cheapen our work. The crowds that gather will soon leave when the excitement is over. Promotion can be effective without belittling our ministry.

In opening a new church there are at least ten areas whereby it might be promoted.

I. Newspaper Advertising

This is a *must*. If for no other reason, you are informing other churches of your presence in the community. Plan your advertisements to communicate your distinctives to people. Be clear as to location and timing of services. You will find a two column "ad" shows up better than a single column, even though the latter may be larger.

II. A Radio Ministry

This is a profitable way to publicize your work. Alex Rockwell of Grace Baptist Church, Charlottetown, Prince Edward Island, made tremendous use of a one minute spot, Monday to Friday, which was aired between 4:45 and 5:00 p.m. He would take a few seconds to refer to an item in the newspaper and then drive home a spiritual throught arising from the news. This minute broadcast became widely known. Church families used it to acquaint their friends with their church and pastor.

"Seek to become known" advises Rudy Holland of Berean Baptist Church of Roanoke Valley, Salem, Virginia. He goes on to say, "Advertise — let people know you are there and state what you believe. People go where they know to go (72:130)." Holland recommends the starting of a radio program as soon as possible. He adds, "The newspaper, television and billboard can be used to attract attention to the church. We must remember every successful business is built upon the fact that it has appealed to the market. The church must do the same without compromising the message (73:130)."

III. A Television Ministry

In a number of cities you can have free or at low cost a cable television program. This comes under the heading of public relations. Many firms are anxious to promote their stations through goodwill programming. Pastor Ron Baxter of Shenstone Baptist Church, Brantford, Ontario, had a weekly program. The station brought their equipment into a small studio set up in the church. Excellent use was made of church members in music, testimonies and the spoken word.

Norman E. Nygaard in his little publication on church advertising says:

> *Many churches are missing the boat because they are apparently still unaware of the fact that the news period on the radio is available to them if they have items which can be used. Many radio stations announce different kinds of meetings. They are eager for news about clubs and organizations and will be glad to make announcements about the doings of your men's club, your youth groups, your women's societies, if you will supply them with the*

*information. You can phone in that information or send it
in on a postal card.*

*If you have a prominent speaker — especially if he or she is
dealing with some controversial subject — you can get
considerable coverage from the radio station and occasionally even from the news broadcasts of your TV
station.*

*You can also get time on a TV station for an interview with
that person. If he has just spoken in your church let that fact
be known. If he is going to speak, that fact should be played
up. The important thing is to work in the name of the
church (102:4).*

IV. Distributing Circulars

Mention has been made in another chapter about distributing
circulars throughout your community. Some do this on a regular
basis. In order to test your area, you could offer a book for those
phoning the church or sending in an addressed card. The book
should be of a nature that would excite attention. In a young
community, for example, the book put out by Zondervan: "I
Want My Marriage to be Better" by Henry Brandt and Phil
Landrum goes over well. The title opens the door for further
contact. There are many such titles available today in an
economical paperback edition. Do this twice a year and the
community will soon get to know that your church cares, yes, it
really cares.

V. Provide a Warm Welcome when New People come

With proper promotion, people are going to come. See that
they get a warm and friendly welcome. This is where your ushers
are part of the promotional work of the church. They can undo in
one minute what you have spent time and dollars to do. On the
other hand, they can reinforce the good impression the
newcomer has of the new church. In a very real way, ushers are
key people in a new church. Their attire and presentation should
be one that draws people in a new work. Their opening greeting
should be warm and real. By all means they should avoid the
mistake Preston Taylor told about that happened in a church in
California. A newcomer appeared at the front door of the church
and the usher greeted and asked where he was from. The
stranger told of his home town. The usher replied: "That's a
terrible town. I heard you have problems with crime etc." If you
can't say something good about a community, say nothing!

It is my understanding that at the First Baptist Church of Van Nuys, California, greeters meet incoming worshippers in the parking lot. Assistance is given with the car doors. Strangers with licenses from outside the community are given an extra warm welcome.

Jerry Falwell includes the following letter in his book on "Capturing a Town for Christ".

Dear Dr. Falwell:

Some time ago I had the privilege of visiting your church on Wednesday evening. I called your secretary the next morning and explained to her why I had come to the church grounds as a dirty bum with a wine bottle in my hands rather than with my customary suit and tie. I left there praising the Lord that somebody in your church would have cared for that kind of man and would have made a determined effort to reach him for Christ. The dear young man who talked to me was so persistent, so interested in me that I barely got away in time to get to my motel, clean myself up and get back for Prayer Meeting.

I want to thank you for leading a church to a place of keen concern for lost people. I have a deep respect and admiration for your ministry.

Devotedly yours,
Roy J. Fish, Th.D.
Professor of Evangelism,
Southwestern Theological Seminary,
Fort Worth, Texas. (18:21)

VI. Use the Sunday School

A Sunday School contest can be a fine means of promoting your work. A useful tool is the publication put out by Christian Life, "How To Win a Sunday School Contest". Suggestions are made for entering a float in a parade and many other ways to get people involved — which can result in growth.

VII. Use Printed Directories

You will find a church directory in the large hotels and motels near your church site. Usually this is free promotion and might well attract new families moving into the community as well as visitors passing through.

VIII. Welcome Newcomers to the Community

Mention has been made about obtaining a Welcome Wagon list. Another feature is to prepare an attractive piece of literature with a pen as materials to be left by the hostess. A follow-up letter and a call would be the way to complete this promotion.

IX. Use the Postal System

Many churches use the mail to write bereaved families, newlyweds and those welcoming a new child. You can obtain names from the daily newspaper. You will want to prepare a well thought through letter and literature for this. Samuel Farina says this about this method:

> *The newspaper also assist our church promotion in a more indirect way. The church has designed special printed pieces which are mailed to persons whose names appear in the newspaper for occasions like weddings, births, honors, promotions, etc. The response to these letters has been warm, and many persons have called to express their appreciation. A few individuals have visited the church as a result of these letters, and some have become members of the church (87:19).*

X. Periodic News of Interest to the General Public.

Giving such news to the press can be effective. Church planter Joe MacDonald of Faith Baptist Church, Port Hope, Ontario, received a national writeup in October, 1977. I was out in Vancouver, British Columbia, about 5500 kilometers from Port Hope when this news item appeared in the Vancouver paper. He had accepted the chairmanship of a movement to fight the Gay people. This humble church planter became known overnight. It goes to show that the evangelical church can have a mass media coverage if what we do is newsworthy.

You will want to follow a few rules about stories for the papers. Have the article well prepared, written as far as possible in typical newspaper style. Make it newsworthy. Include prominent names when possible. This is most important in rural and small town communities. Getting to know the religious editor is a good policy.

Norman Nygaard gives the following special directions about the way to write articles so that they will be considered for publication:

> *Don't try to put a heading on your article. This is the*

*editor's job and even though you know how to write a
heading don't do it.*

*Always leave the top third of a sheet of paper on which your
news article is written with no writing whatsoever. If you
want the article to go into a certain issue of the paper you
can put a release date in the upper left-hand corner with
some notation as this — 'Do not release until Feb. 28th'. If
this is done run as close to the top of the sheet as possible.*

*Always triple-space. The cardinal sin in newspaper writing
is to single-space an article. The reason for triple-spacing, of
course, is to allow editorial blue-penciling.*

*Always tell the entire story in your lead sentence. The
material which follows is merely an elaboration of the lead.
The lead sentence should capture the interest of the reader
and make him want to go on and read the rest of the story.*

Articles should always be written in the third person.

*Newspaper articles preferably consist of three, five, or seven
paragraphs (94:5,6).*

Delegate the job of newspaper promotion if you have an able
writer in the church. You might be wise to train a writer, or make
it possible for such a one to receive training. Perhaps your church
would cover the cost of an evening course for one who would take
this seriously.

Letters of commendation to the editor are appreciated.

In preparing this section the account came to me of an interesting human drama. A church purchased a new car for their
pastor as a Christmas gift. The presentation was made by driving
it down the centre aisle of the auditorium. Needless to say it hit
the headlines. I am not suggesting such dramatic experiences but
that we make known accounts of human drama (87:17).

Example of a Church Planter
Who knows How to Promote

Pastor Larry Johnson founded the Kawartha Baptist Temple,
Peterborough, Ontario, in the fall of 1974. He started with just
his own family. He did not have people, workers or finances! In
the first three years the church has seen nearly 600 professions of
faith. The congregation has erected a large edifice on a choice
19.7 acre site on the main highway leading into the city. On
special Sundays the attendance have exceeded 900. One Sunday
the total offerings were $17,942.10. God has been so good to the
pastor and people.

One of the keys to the growth of the church has been the

advertising directed by Pastor Johnson. The Kawartha Baptist Temple is clearly the most promoted church in Peterborough. The larbe billboard on Highway 28 greets everyone entering the city. The church carries the largest paid "ad" on the church page so that people will read it first. It is the only church that runs a one column block ad in the Telephone Directory of the Yellow Pages.

Two regular publications are produced. Weekly the KBT Bus News is distributed by the bus captains as they visit on the five bus routes. *Faith In Action* is published quarterly. Here the pastor makes use of his men. One is Ken Holman, a commercial artist, who designs the papers and assists in other unique promotional fliers.

A successful advertising campaign must be planned. Larry Johnson seeks to plan a year ahead. He states that one should have adequate time to think through all the details.

Proper promotion in the local church does not cost, it pays, according to Larry Johnson. Because of advertising, new people are constantly sitting under the sound of the gospel who would not have come otherwise. Many get saved, baptized and join the church and thus start serving the Lord, including bringing their tithes. The most effective promotional materials are the ones that result in the most people getting right with God. Ideas that fail to generate enthusiasm for reaching the lost are not used the second time.

What about criticism? Yes, the Kawartha Baptist Temple is criticized. Larry Johnson responds to this by saying that the liberal churches who hate Bible Christianity and whose attendances are dwindling and also the charismatic churches who cannot explain how the church is growing faster than they are "without the Holy Spirit" are constantly speaking against the church. Larry Johnson is anxious to respond positively to helpful constructive criticism but most of the criticism that is leveled is not of that variety. His determination is to please God rather than men and he will continue to do all that is humanly possible to please Him even if it means alienating critics.

From the way the church advertises, one would expect a considerable budget. Actually, less than 4% of their unified budget is spent on promotion. This is not much for the returns.

Larry Johnson believes in promotion with Scriptural motivation. To him there is nothing unspiritual about proper promotion. He has found that many professing fundamental, Bible-believing pastors and people fail to grasp the vast spiritual potential in Biblical promotion or are afraid of the ever present critics. Promotion as it applies to the local New Testament church must be aligned with both motivation and goals that are Christ-exalting and unselfish! In other words, a promotional event must be in line with the teaching of Scripture and must honour God. Since it is God's will that people be saved (2 Peter 3:9; 1 Tim. 2:3,4; Acts 17:30) he is determined that he will do anything that is not unscriptural or selfish to get multitudes under the sound of the gospel and as many people saved as possible. Was not this Paul's motivation when he declared: "I am made all things to all men, that I might by all means save some (1 Cor. 9:20)"?

It would be difficult, Larry Johnson believes, to argue against using promotion in the local church from a scriptural standpoint without arguing with the Lord Jesus Himself. Miracles in the New Testament and the promised rewards at the judgment seat of Christ are clear examples of Biblical promotion to reach spiritual ends. Miracles were used to bring people to Christ. The coming judgment of believers should lead to consistent, fruitful Christian living today.

Larry Johnson does not believe God will bless promotion that is only geared to build a bigger Sunday School than everyone else. There is nothing wrong with having a large Sunday School. God is honoured in doing things in a big way. But, if your desire to grow is selfish, be prepared to fail. However, God will use promotion if the motivation for such is soul winning.

So, in launching a new church, "Don't hide your light" but advertise well. Let the people know what you are doing and where. Use all means honouring His name, to make known the glorious news that Jesus Christ saves.

Chapter 12

USE ME OR LOSE ME

A church planter, like Barnabas, will seek to touch lives and involve people in the work. There's a significant thought in Acts 9:26,27:

> And when Saul was come to Jerusalem, he assayed to join himself to the disciples: but they were all afraid of him, and believed not that he was a disciple. But Barnabas took him, and brought him to the apostles, and declared unto them how he had seen the Lord in the way, and that he had spoken to Him, and how he had preached boldly at Damascus.

Can you hear some believers in verse 26 saying: "We have never done it this way before"? Yet Barnabas, with a resolute heart, sought and brought Saul who later became the greatest church planter of all time.

In Acts 15:36-39, Luke records the dramatic disagreement between Paul and Barnabas concerning John Mark. Yes, John Mark had made a mistake, but Barnabas, recognizing his potential as a servant of the Lord, wanted to give him another chance. As a result, God raised up in the person of John Mark an evangelist, and the early church was blessed.

I. Biblical Principle of Responsibility

Barnabas applied the principle of responsibility. In doing so he multiplied his ministry by touching and using people. This is a biblical principle church planters should seek to cultivate. Just as Barnabas trusted Paul, so we must show confidence in others. Just as Barnabas took Mark with him on his missionary journey, so we must take people with us in visitation evangelism and other avenues of Christian service in order to develop their God-given abilities.

Basically, a New Testament church is made up of believers banded together for worship and witness. Paul says in I Cor. 3:9: "We are labourers together with God". Starting a church is not a one man job, but rather the work of a leader, under God, seeking to mould new converts and older Christians into a working unit.

There are two extremes in the involvement of people. On one side a pastor might refuse to recognize gifts in his people until he has been associated with them for several years. I have known several church planters who have started new churches and, five years later, still do not have one deacon. It was not because the churches did not have male members. The potential was there, but the pastors were looking for ready-made leadership. They failed to appreciate the ultimate worth of their co-workers and, therefore, could not trust them with responsible positions in the church. The excuse was that the church did not have qualified men to serve as deacons. This might well be the case but, after five years, one wonders if the church has had a qualified pastor! One of the functions of the pastor, according to Ephes. 4:11,12 is to develop leadership within the local church: "And He gave some, apostles; and some, prophets; and some, evangelists; and some, pastors and teachers; for the perfecting of the saints, for the work of the ministry, for the edifying of the body of Christ".

The other extreme is to appoint people to important positions before they are ready. A pastor may be over anxious to see a spot filled and so will take whoever is available. Likewise, a willing individual may step forward and offer himself for a particular position. You could be making a mistake if you appoint him without due consideration of his background.

Somewhere between these two extremes there is a balance. It is true that unless you use a person you might lose him. This brings us to consider the important aspect of the participation of members in a local church. How can we get people to participate?

One way is to follow the biblical principle of responsibility. In Matt. 25:21 our Lord outlines the method of developing dependable workers: "Well done, thou good and faithful servant: thou hast been faithful over a few things, I will make thee ruler over many things". Seek out specific positions where an individual may exercise his leadership ability. As his workmanship proves valuable, increase the area of responsibility. Elmer Towns tells about Pastor James Singleton of the Tri-City Baptist Church, Temple, Arizona and how he developed Sunday School teachers and leaders:

> *From the very beginning Singleton realized that Sunday School would be the agency to build a church, 'reaching . . . teaching. . . winning. . . training'. He met weekly with all the teachers, giving them instruction in both content and methodology. He personally recruited all teachers, stressing qualifications: salvation, church membership, tithing, attendance, pupil visitation, and separation from the world. Today he cautions young preachers: 'It is a mistake to relax standards in the early days of a church because of pressure to get a church started, with a view to strengthening the teaching staff in the future'. Then he notes: "I will sacrifice fast growth for stability and wait for God to send workers. We don't want to plant seeds that will damage the church in the future' (73:62).*

II. Motivate People

Motivate people to participate in the church program. What is motivation? Motivation is that which causes us to get things done! Webster's dictionary says: "Something (as a need or desire) that causes a person to act". Now motivation is a complex subject. The following from Hilgard and Atkinson will give some idea as to the complexity of it:

> *Everyday experiences teach us a good deal about motivated behaviour. We are aware of those who set high goals and then work strenuously to reach them. Athletic competition provides ready examples, with broken records and Olympic gold medals serving as signs of success. But non-athletes, too, set difficult goals and work hard to reach them: artists, musicians, scientists, businessmen. At the other extreme we find those who are apathetic and seem unable to make the effort to plan ahead or to compete enough in daily activities to sustain a participative role in society. We find still others who give up lives of ease and security to face hardships in order to serve the needy in far-off places. People obviously differ widely in the activities that they find most satisfying and in the energy that they invest in the activities they choose (34:312).*

The above quotation, although written for a cross section of our society, applies to those gathered into new churches. Thus, motivation is an important aspect and must be part of our ministry. Too often there has been a tendency to nag, push or shame people into action. Whereas, by following the biblical approach, it is possible to grasp ways of leading people into action — action that can be satisfying to them and profitable to the church.

Douglas MacGregor's theory of "X" and "Y" has been helpful. According to this theory the need to produce is inherent in people. It is the role of the pastor to set up the necessary atmosphere or environment to enable members to function to their utmost potential.

The writer is deeply conscious of the fact that behind the above there is the most important aspect — the spiritual. One must remember the way Paul motivated leaders of the first century, according to Rom. 12:1: "I beseech you therefore brethren, by the mercies of God, that ye present your bodies a living sacrifice, holy, acceptable unto God, which is your reasonable service". You note that he motivated believers to dedication through Jesus Christ. This is spiritual leadership at its best. Kenneth Gangel catches the spirit when he suggests:

> One of the beautiful words describing the work of the church is the word dikanos. It means 'service' and is precisely what Christ did for His disciples in that upper room. The question seems to be rhetorical: Who is most important, the waiter or the dinner guest? Obvious answer: the dinner guest, of course! But wait a minute, who is the guest and who is the waiter at the Last Supper? Answer: 'I am among you as He that serveth'. Conclusion: New Testament leadership is not flashy public relations and platform personality, but humble service to the group (24:13).

III. Know your People and their Gifts

Another way to bring about participation is to get to know your people. Robert Dale sent a questionaire to new people asking them for information that would assist him in his ministry to them. Others request that each new member or prospect complete and return a talent survey sheet. It is helpful to have a stewardship chairman responsible for setting up a file according to positions. In this way, when a clerk is needed, the stewardship chairman should be able to furnish the name of another person who could do the job. You will find a suggested stewardship survey form in the Appendix.

IV. Train your People

Training will help get people to participate. People want to learn. Often the problem is that pastors get so involved with starting a church that they do not take time to disciple believers. Possibly our schools have failed to emphasize this as Harold Longenecker suggests:

> It seems clear that many of our training institutions have put the cart before the horse. We have been teaching men to go out with the intent to build churches when we should have trained them to go out to win men to Christ and equip them for effective witness (44:80).

An illustration of training was brought to my attention in a letter that came to my desk from Pastor Don Robins of Lower Sackville, Nova Scotia. Mention was made of his desire to build a soul-winning congregation. But how could this be done? Read the following from his letter and see if you can suggest a better way! "Before I started this church, I decided that I wanted to train my people to be soul winners. The best way I know to train them is to take one with me, train him, and then the two of us will each take someone else and train him. Last evening Brother Wayne Vail, one of our laymen who seems to have some potential in this area, and I went out soul-winning. Although we have been out twice, he has not yet had the privilege of personally winning a soul to Christ. Please pray that he will have this opportunity soon."

V. Develop a Team Spirit

This brings about participation. Paul, in writing to the Philippian Church, commends them for their active participation in the ministry. In Phil. 1:7 he said that all the members were active in the ministry. One can well imagine the impact of Evangelicals if every member were active. Yet you can strive for this goal in a new church. Every member should be considered a minister or missionary of the church, called of God, and working together as a team. This gives dignity to membership and the sense of belonging to an active growing church. It helps an indi idual to feel wanted. Dr. George Crane's syndicated column, "The Worry Clinic", once stated that underneath every person's clothes, could one but see it, is a flashing neon sign which says: "I want to feel important! (83:)"

A word needs to be said about reaching men for Christ and getting them involved in a new church. At times a church planter is tempted to look at numbers and therefore spend a major portion of his time gathering children and youth. This is important but, if it is done at the expense of not having time for men, then it is putting the cart before the horse. Andrew Blackwood has well said: "Every pastor knows the need of attracting men, one by one, and in groups. For his sake, he ought to mingle with them freely, as well as with women and children. For the good of the men also he should seek them out as their pastor and guide. Ere long he should become 'a friend that sticketh closer than a brother' (9)."

A number of church planters make it a point to arrange for one or two luncheon engagements a week with prospective laymen. Seek to find out the best time to visit men, either in the evening or, if one is on shift work, take time during the afternoon. Take with you selected books that especially appeal to men. "Born Again" by Charles Colson was one that really spoke to men, as Colson traced his experience with the former President of the United States, Richard Nixon.

VI. What about the Use of Non-Members

There's a real temptation to get people involved by using them, and thus hoping to hold them. Could this be manipulation? Have you ever been in a restaurant which had a sign: "Our cook eats here!" Really, if your new church is worth serving, it is worth joining.

VII. Over-Working People

One word of caution to be given concerning the over-working of people. This is a problem with many growing churches. There are many things to do and few hands to do them. As a result we are apt to over-load good willing members. This can hurt the growth pattern. Over-worked members cannot do every job as well as it should be done. It might hurt the family life in that you take a husband or wife away from their children several nights a week. I have seen members leave a church because they were expected to serve in too many positions. It is better to give each position a certain value as it relates to time consumption. Divide the jobs up, getting every member involved. Keep records showing the jobs that are being done and seek to pass the work around.

Does participation work today? M. Wendell Belew tells of a small group of twenty-two Christians in the inner city of Worcester, Massachusetts:

They were motivated from the beginning with a desire to communicate through involvement. Their involvement was incredible for so small a group.

Their worship service was a kind of strategy meeting where their plans for involvement were involved with God. Each member saw himself in the light of what talents he had and would use. They studied the community's needs and determined how they would relate redemptively to these. The needs were many. There were dope addicts, elderly people in a modern high-rise apartment across the street from the church house. There was a college, multiracial groups, acres of low-rent tenements, hundreds of children playing on the streets, business people, and older youth without purpose. Like leaven, the church began to grow. (5:48)

This is what the gospel of Christ can do when a group of believers seek to proclaim the Good News. And this is one of the important functions of a local church, to reach the community with the Word of God.

Example of a Church Planter Who knows how to use People

Does participation work? I asked church planter Thorald Marsaw about his plans for the new church he has started in Agincourt, a community in the eastern part of Toronto. Prior to this Thorald Marsaw was a Lieutenant Colonel in the Canadian Armed Forces. He took an early retirement to go into the ministry. The influence of his military background is seen in his desire to get his people personally involved in the work.

Many church planters use job descriptions. Thorald Marsaw feels they can be helpful for key slots, but they can become an administrative burden and will often discourage some beginners because they may seem overpowering. He thinks the best way to define what a job entails is by On-Job-Training (OJT). When a person sees how another can cope with all that must be done in a given amount of time, the tendency is to think how he could improve on what he has seen, not to worry about the magnitude of the load.

According to Thorald Marsaw, the pastor should know what he wants done and look for the one who best qualifies to do the job. He thinks that the average person has more talent than he needs for a given task, the problem is getting him to see that he does.

With his military background he is not afraid to put his members to work. He teaches that just as personal skill will be lost if it is not exercised, so too will people. Even those that are not inclined to "volunteer" to serve will be lost if they are not used. Oh, they may occupy a chair or pew, but they are to all intents and purposes on the shelf and hence of little value. He believes in shaking the shelf . . . things cannot get worse.

He offers a good word about overworking people, a lesson he learned the hard way. He suggests that people need to be stretched but not overworked. They need to be challenged to reach out and expand. Overworked people do not do a good job, and they are easily discouraged and frustrated. Overwork someone for a year, and you will burn him out. From then on he will run for cover in order to avoid involvement.

This church planter does not ask for volunteers. He works on a one to one basis all the time. He is developing an opportunity list which has a descriptive scale on which the members check off their interest level for specific areas of service. Should you choose to use such an opportunity list when interviewing folk for church membership, it would be advisable to have them fill it out before the interview so that you can use the completed form as the basis for a discussion on service opportunities and interests.

He aims to show people how. This is especially necessary in respect to visitation and evangelism. Time is the enemy of intent, but quality performance eventually depends on know how. We must show them.

Interaction and fellowship amongst leaders is encouraged. He feels that a pastor should attend as many functions and activities as possible to show his interest and to encourage quality preparation. He likes to quote from Share: "People don't do what you expect, but what you inspect (68: Step 5).

Like Barnabas in the Bible, he is able to give people a second opportunity. His philosophy is that you should not let what you know about someone, lead you to discount his potential. The path to purpose in the Christian walk is built on the stones of opportunity.

Once someone says — yes, "demand" performance. He tends to discourage the "volunteer" philosophy which relegates Christian work to the lowest priority.

He is not afraid of sharing the pulpit with his men. In fact he seeks to develop others. He devises incentives. He says: "Don't guard your privileges of service too jealousy. . . every church of any consequence has more than one preacher in it. . . find him."

He claims that two thirs of any call is the recognition of a need and a measured capacity to meet that need. He does not stress so much: "God, would you have me in that service?" but "Lord, is there any reason why I shouldn't be?"

This church planter is convinced that the church would be a much better place if the people would accept a number of military principles in the governing of their service. He suggests that that is expressly why the Lord calls us a mighty army and used so many military illustrations. He gives the following principles of war:

1. Selection and maintainance of the aim (define the principle aim and test all the others against it);
2. Offensive action (don't sit back);
3. Economy of effort (especially account for our time — plan your work and work your plan);
4. Concentration of force (don't spread too thin — define your priorities);
5. Flexibility (the world is changing and we need to recognize that fact)
6. Cooperation (Why are Evangelicals competing so vigorously?)

He teaches that a leader must be willing to get his hands dirty, work in the rain, etc. Indeed, he must demonstrate a capacity to do all non-specialist ministries he is calling upon others to perform. The more difficult the situation the more important is his personal presence. But do not take over if you can avoid it — show them how, help, but let them get on with it. Encourage, and do not be afraid to push a little (lovingly).

He cites a practical example of when he was a member of Central Baptist Church, Victoria, British Columbia. He was responsible for Christian Service Brigade. Two weeks every summer was spent visiting the men of the church for, in Christian Service Brigade, there is a role for every Christian man. In two years the group moved from a total involvement of under 35 men and boys to a place where the church had 34 leaders running a two company battalion and four stockades. The "practical" key to success was personal contact and spreading the load. One more leader was added than the recognized minimum to each group and a "Fire Brigade" of former leaders was also formed who would answer an emergency call at minimum notice. Then the team programmed imaginatively and God blessed it.

Is it any wonder that in the first two months of his new church in Agincourt he had over seventy indicating interest in Bible study? He has projected a congregation of several hundreds

within a decade. This is leadership through involvement of
members. "Go and do thou likewise."

Chapter 13

PUT YOUR BEST FOOT FOREWARD

It makes sense to put your best foot forward. Dr. Leonard Zunin once said: "What two people communicate during their first four minutes of contact is so crucial that it will determine whether strangers will remain strangers or become acquaintances, friends, lovers or lifetime mates (105:1)." If you are going to influence people, you must to a certain degree, draw them to yourself.

Seven areas have an influence on our public relations. Study these areas, making the necessary changes, and your public relations will be notably different.

I. Accept Yourself

Self-confidence is a necessity in a church planter. You must know yourself, accept yourself and be yourself. You get to know yourself by listening to others around you, your spouse and close friends. If you are open they will help you to better understand yourself. Accepting yourself is one of the first steps in loving others. Be yourself is a manifestation of sincerity. If God wanted you to be another Haddon Spurgeon, He would have so ordained it. Barbara Walters tells about interviewing Mrs. Eugene McCarthy during the time her husband was seeking the Democratic presidential nomination in the United States. In response to the question how she was reacting to her sudden fame and attention, replied, that she had been nervous at first, but cured herself one day by deciding: "I am the way I am; I look the way I look; I am my age (104:7)".

II. Personal Appearance is Important

Hygiene and apparel speak louder than words. A daily bath, deodorants, breath tablets and a routine dental checkup can go a long way to help in the matter of personal hygiene. While clothes do not make a man, they certainly help! Cheap clothes, in the long run, might well be more expensive. Take advantage of the annual sales in January and July to pick up quality clothing at discount prices. You will feel more comfortable and will look sharper.

Hair plays a prominent part in your appearance. Unkept hair speaks of carelessness. This might well carry over into other areas of an individual's personality.

There are a host of little things that are important. Dirty finger nails, unpolished shoes, baggy and outdated clothes and way-out styles also speak of your personality. James T. Mangan suggests "They always judge the book by its cover (102:21)". Nothing can take the place of a good front cover. One publisher told me that the cover has a major part in selling a book. "A good personal appearance will get any man by, with scarcely any aid from any other quality, but all other qualities put together have a hard job getting any man by, if he doesn't make a good personal appearance (102:21)."

III. A Winsome Personality Helps

A repulsive personality will not draw positive people. A full uninteresting personality will not attract zestful lively folks. A withdrawn shy individual will not lead outgoing forward moving people. An enthusiastic church planter will add a dimension that is needed in starting a new church.

Dale Carnegie gave a stirring talk on the power of enthusiasm. He got so excited during his talk, he threw a chair up against the wall and broke off one of its legs (8:7). Now I am not suggesting that you take a pulpit chair and do the same, but there is real value in being sold on your work and expressing it in an enthusiastic way.

IV. Courtesy and Gratitude make a Beautiful Pair

A church planter should be the model of a gentleman. Good manners indicate controlled behaviour. The syndicated columnist, Sidney Harris, tells the story of accompanying his friend to a news stand. The friend greeted the newsman very courteously, but in return received gruff and discourteous service. Accepting the newspaper which was shoved rudely in his direction, the friend of Harris politely smiled and wished the newspaper man a nice weekend. As the two friends walked down the street, the columnist asked: "Does he always treat you so rudely?" "Yes, unfortunately he does." "And are you always so polite and friendly to him?" "Yes, I am." "Why are you so nice to him when he is so unfriendly to you?" "Because I don't want him to decide how I am going to act (103:38,39)." Courtesy is always in season. With the church planter it begins at home and branches out to the church and the community.

Gratitude, David says: "Is comely for the upright (Psalm 33:1)." It is expected, that a pastor, of all people, show a genuine thankful spirit. Yet there have been times when this has been lacking. One pastor sent a love gift of $500 to a new church in response to a request for help. Although the cheque was received and cashed by the church, no word of appreciation was ever sent. Most church planters would be glad to send a dozen letters for such a generous gift! It would seem that the above church planter just took monetary gifts for granted. Take time to write thank you notes. Take time to express your gratitude for work accomplished by teachers, ushers, and others engaged with you in planting a church.

V. Recognize and Remember People

The church is people. We are in a ministry to people. It is most important you remember a name when it is given you. Say it over in your mind. If it is a difficult name, have the person spell it for you. Try to connect the name with something. When people come for the first time in response to door to door visitation, they will sense the genuineness of your concern for them as you call them by name and remind them of something said during your visit in their home.

Remember your people and their special days. Anniversaries and birthdays are significant. A personal note from you will show you care. Do not forget the children. Even little ones appreciate a pastor who sends a greeting.

Rev. Rodney Gould, for many years pastor of the Calvary Baptist Church, Cedar Rapids, Iowa, made it routine at the first of each month to take time with his wife to write birthday and anniversary greetings to the membership. Dr. Donald Loveday, who for 25 years served as pastor of the Central Baptist

Church, Brantford, Ontario, would drop a personal note to his members on their birthdays. He would recall a certain act of kindness or a special function carried out and commend the member for the same.

One of the most blessed experiences for parents is to give birth to a baby. This is where you can show interest and a concern for the new child. "Pastor, we received your letter to Susan. It will long be remembered." This comment came to me from a happy mother of a new born infant daughter. Usually, letters from a pastor or the church cause little comment from church members. Letters to infants create real interest. In many cases it will be the first letter received by the infant. Consider composing a letter and send it to each new born child. It is wise to obtain the name of the child and to send it to his home address. You will find this extra touch meaningful to the parents. Anything that touches their 'precious little bundle of love' touches them. A letter to the newborn can often be the key to a more vital ministry to the parents. See Appendix 6 for a sample letter.

Another way is to visit the hospital when the father is present and have the couple join their hands in prayer as you thank God with them for their new bundle of love.

VI. Develop the Skill of a Conversationalist

It is both pleasurable and profitable to carry on a conversation with others. It's an art every church planter should cultivate. There are many things to talk about besides the weather! It is not wise to compliment a stranger about his clothes. You can do this with your members, but let a stranger get to know you before remarking on personal items. Carry on a conversation that is positive. It was Jacques Barzun who said that: "Educated people talk about ideas, semi-educated about events, and un-educated about people." If possible, plan your conversation ahead of time, think of what might interest your contacts. Look up background material on their ministries. Recall previous visits.

VII. Develop Friendships

It is recorded in Proverbs 18:24: "A man that hath friends must shew himself friendly". Many people are looking for genuine friendship. In this age of decreased interpersonal dependence, there is not the same outward need for sociability. For example, television occupies a major portion of the evening in the lives of many families, furthermore, in our development of mechanization, there is not the same interdependence of man at work. Yet, man is a social creature. There is a place for the church planter to provide on the part of the new church, a friendship, that can be both meaningful and helpful.

Satisfying human relationships can be realized only to the degree that genuine understanding exists. It is important that one seeks to understand personality differences. Co-operate with them rather than struggle against them. People are interesting. You are interesting. A pastor cannot be an island living alone in the world of mankind. He must go out and "Put his best foot forward". One of the finest compliments of a church planter should be: "He loves people".

In this day when people use people and love things, the church planter should love people and use things. There are trends toward a rootless society. This can be a very cold world. People are in need of people who are ready to develop genuine friendships. This can be a real help in planting a church.

Example of a Church Planter who knows P.R.

One fine example of a church planter known for public relations is Pastor James Rendle of the Bradford Baptist Church, Bradford, Ontario. His overt behaviour is a reflection of his heart. First and forement he has recognized the need of being right with the Lord. Before he and Anna his wife made any important move, they sought the face of God for wisdom and direction.

One afternoon the telephone rang. Jim Rendle had just closed the envelope to a letter to a church inviting him to be their pastor. For some reason he did not have complete peace about going and thus deferred his decision and declined later. "Hello,' he answered. He was surprised to hear my voice and doubly surprised to hear about the opportunity to launch a new work in Bradford. Normally one would not think twice about this after deferring another opportunity just moments earlier. Yet he sensed that perhaps God was in it.

Many questions came to his mind. As a pastor grows older, there is a hesitancy to "launch out into the deep". Why leave a known situation or an established church to begin a new work? There are many unknown factors. What kind of reception will one receive in a new community? Will the nucleus band together in a viable unity? Will the church grow sufficiently to support the pastor? Will his family fit into this new situation? It is much easier to remain in an established church with an adequate salary, among friends, but is it God's will? And God's will is foremost! James Rendle, like so many other church planters, discovered that when a person senses God's will and launches forth with a commitment to that will, God does the impossible. Jim has found the words of Jeremiah 32:27 a source of deep comfort: "Behold, I am the Lord, the God of all flesh, is there anything too hard for me?" As he looks back over his work he can say: "Lord, there is nothing too hard for you".

Once the heart is right with God things tend to fit into place. One step led to another in his work of church planting. He wanted to "Put his best foot forward" and so he sought for a house in the heart of the community where he was planning to start a church. This would enable him to identify with the community. Many church planters make the mistake of living several miles away from their field of ministry.

He next prepared an attractive folder to announce opening services. He paid a little more but the publication communicated the quality of services and ministry planned. He knew the value of contacting the whole town at once so motivated members from the parent church, Victory Baptist Church, Newmarket to assist with the distribution.

There is nothing like having the mass media behind your new work. He made it a point to visit the Bradford Witness newspaper. The writer of the community and religious news was Carol Simone. His first visit lasted an hour and a half. The Simones live in the Holland Marsh area just a couple of miles from Bradford. It turned out that Carol was a Christian but her husband Andy had not made a commitment to Christ and, in fact, was rather disgusted with many things that happen within churches. He seldom attended any church. On Father's Day in June, 1977 the Simone family came to the Bradford Baptist Church. God touched Andy's heart and he has now become a Christian and is faithful to the services.

The spirit of understanding in the heart of Jim Rendle is seen from the types of messages prepared and presented. In a new work there are people who come from various denominational backgrounds. It is important to establish them in the Word and guide them in Baptist beliefs. Recognizing that many would not understand the type of vocabulary used in a fundamental church, he gave a series on "Words You Should Know". He dealt with redemption, reconciliation, propitiation and justification. He wanted people to know what is involved in salvation and the glory of the cross.

He tries to meet the needs of the people in his preaching. Consequently, because of the charismatic influence in the area and on television, he gave a series on the Holy Spirit. Excellent questions were given in the Question Box which he sought to answer on Sunday evenings. In this way he does not avoid issues but tactfully meets them with the Word of God.

As is so often the case with new churches, people visit from other fundamental churches. He seeks to work with these other churches and not be a threat to them. He desires people to unite with Bradford Baptist Church because they have been led of the Lord and not pressured by coercion. Thus he discusses freely with other pastors anyone who may be disgruntled.

He takes care of details that mean much in his public relations. One example is he had the church take out special insurance for using the school building, in case of accident. Most would take this for granted and expect to make use of the school insurance. He maintains a wonderful relationship with the school officials and custodians and as a result finds them most cooperative. At Christmas time the church gives the school custodians fruit baskets in appreciation of their co-operation.

Concerned with making a good impression on new people he works through the Welcome Wagon Hostess. In this way he is able to introduce the church to new residents.

The Bradford Baptist Church started in the home of Mr. & Mrs. John Waters on November 2, 1976. To the amazement of all concerned no one arrived at the first meeting except the Waters and myself. The second Bible study the following week proved to be a little more encouraging with four new people making a total of eight. One year later the group had grown to almost a hundred. In addition, an offer was made and accepted for the purchase of two acres of land. The church was at the same time organized with five deacons and an able Sunday School teaching staff by the date of the first annual meeting.

Mrs. Ruth Coutts, the temporary clerk, read a brief history of the church at the Recognition Service and concluded with the following statement: "Truly the Lord has engineered the work all the way and it is our earnest prayer that it may never be any other way".

Pastor Rendle tells about the Holland Marsh area just outside Bradford. This is a fertile place for growing onions, lettuce, cabbage, carrots, celery, brussel sprouts, broccoli and other vegetables. Surely this was God's timing in the planting of a New Testament church. With the dynamic vitamins of the Holy Spirit working in the lives of His own people, the church in Bradford is bound to grow.

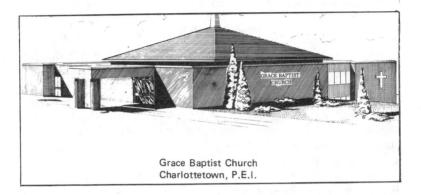

Chapter 14

Grace Baptist Church
Charlottetown, P.E.I.

PROPERTY, AN ASSET

Property is an asset and determines to a certain degree the ultimate potential of a new church. Although land costs are high in certain areas, land itself is a valuable asset for a new work. Strategic planning is a necessity in determining the general areas to be served by the new church. After this comes the choosing of an actual location where the church will be placed. Hence you will purchase the most suitable land available to serve the strategic plan. Getting a parcel of cheap land at the cost of a strategic location, in the long run, is false economy and poor planning.

I. Pick it Early

Land acquisition should be high on the list of priorities in starting a new church. Some church planters have waited three to four years before choosing a site. It is much better to get into a community and secure a desirable piece of property soon thereafter. A large attractive sign will give evidence that the church is becoming established.

People will give to a building fund but they will give more to something they can see, such as property. Church planters have experienced increased offerings when they have a loan to repay, whether it be on a building site or an edifice.

If the first site turns out, for one reason or another, to be unsuitable, it can be traded or sold for a better one. However, you have gained through the appreciation in value of the original site making it easier to purchase a more suitable property.

II. Pick the Right Size

The size of site will be determined to a certain degree by whether the new church is to be a community or regional congregation. A community church will serve one or two neighbourhoods. A small town would fit this classification too. An acre or so should meet the needs of a typical community church. A regional church is one which will serve several miles in all directions. Here a large acreage will be needed to meet the needs of many people.

One example of a community church is the Port of Fellowship Baptist in Port Elgin, Ontario. This town has a population of 3500. The church secured a one acre site, ideally located on the main artery.

Churchill Heights Baptist Church, Toronto, is a regional church. It will serve a population of over 100,000 in the east part of the city. A new $1,200,000 edifice opened in the spring of 1978 on a choice three and a half acre site. However, an agreement was worked out with the municipal offices for the church to use the parking facilities of the adjoining shopping centre. This church includes families who drive from ten to fifteen miles. This is in keeping with the church growth concept of Medford Jones:

> *The constituent area of the church is a defined geographical area surrounding the church site from which the church draws most of its membership and at which the program of the church is aimed. The constituent area usually varies between a three and six mile radius of the church site, and encompasses an area not more than 20 minutes driving time from the church site. (100:20).*

In buying an adequate site, buy with the future in mind. Will there be additional ministries of the local church such as a Christian day school or a residence for senior citizens or other enterprises?

III. Provide for Off-Street Parking

Off-street parking is a necessity in many communities. An adequate site means that sufficient parking is available for a growing congregation. Robert Schuller says: "The first thing you need before anything else is surplus parking. Get them to park their cars, put their keys in their pockets and you have them for a Sunday morning (68:21)."

Local ordinances differ from one urban area to another. However, the average is to provide one parking space for every five seats in the church auditorium.

IV. Accessibility is Important

Accessibility is another important feature in a church site. One pastor advertises in the paper the motto: "Hard to find, but worth finding". This is like saying: "We have a good thing if you can find it." In looking for a new church building in a community of several thousand, I was directed down one street to its dead end and there, next to the railroad tracks, was the church edifice. To make matters worse, during the Sunday morning service, a freight train passed towards the close of my sermon. The congregation purchased the site for a small sum and in doing so crippled the permanent growth of the church. Nine years have passed and that congregation is still small and struggling.

Accessibility does not necessarily call for a church in the heart of a community, unless it is a limited work. A location near a main road, if not on a main artery, is highly desirable. Robert Schuller says:

> *Shopping centres are located at major highway interchanges or at the junction of the major streets or highways. Logically the first thing a business needs is a good room for a place of business. It is obvious that the best product can not be sold and will not be bought if people can't get their hands on it. So, in putting the church within the heart of the community the church was violating a fundamental principal of retailing-accessibility. (68:19)*

In speaking of poor locations, M. Wendell Belew says: "Many churches have found themselves strangled by their locations. It may have been that the church made a poor choice in locating itself in the beginning. Or highways, railroads, and encroaching businesses strangled its growth. (5:24)".

V. Visibility is an Advertiser

Visibility is the best sign your church can erect. You can have signs pointing to your church edifice, but the actual visibility of the building is best. Elmer Towns suggests that: "The church should be visible, place the building on a slight elevation so it can be seen from the street with the most traffic. Many churches have used signs to attract attention, but studies show that the public remembers the building better than any other form of media. (72:144)

It is best when you combine accessibility with visibility. Ezra Jones gives the following helpful suggestions:

> *The church should be approchable from at least two directions. Preferably, the site will be at the corner of a major thoroughfare and a cross street where traffic signals make it possible for people on both sides of the thoroughfare to get to the church safely. A church thus located can be seen by new residents in the community and allows ingress and egress to the parking area from two directions. (39:80)*

Senior citizens, wheel chair members and others with severe physical handicaps appreciate as few steps as possible. Give consideration to topography. Ezra Jones observes that: "Some churches have found it possible to have ground-level entrance ways on as many as three levels because of the slope of the property. (39:7)

VI. Things to Consider in Site Selection

Elmer Towns suggests that the church planter should drive through the neighbourhood and take note:

1. The public schools
2. The shopping centres
3. The existing churches
4. The price and value of homes
5. The projection of new homes
6. The size of building lots
7. Topography
8. Water, sewage, and gas connections
9. Industrial and other barriers in the neighbourhood
10. The main arteries and thoroughfares
11. In addition, get the zoning ordinances in the city to determine restrictions on a proposed church (72:143).

In recent years some churches have purchased several acres from 2 to 5 miles outside the city. Here they found the cost factor was not as severe. The only problem is that generally speaking, people drive inward to a community. It is seeking to reverse the flow of traffic when you locate away from the population.

There are several things to look into when considering your site. Are utilities available? What about public transit? What is the shape of the site? Who are your neighbours? What is the density of the area?

In the typical suburban community you use the formula of 3.5 persons in a residence. In a low-cost housing development use 4 persons as a formula. Apartment buildings, use 3 for mixed housing and 2 if the structures are only for adults.

Soil tests serve a real purpose. In one city the people discovered they could not build a basement because of the rock foundation below the surface, unless they were willing to pay an enormous cost. As Ezra Jones says: "Soil tests should be made to assure that the property will support the buildings and that septic tanks may be used where needed. A church in a Detroit suburb once had to spend one hundred thousand dollars on cement pilings because of poor soil conditions. (39:83)

VII. Legal Counsel is Important

It is understood that you will work through a lawyer in all legal matters. The pastor should let the officers of the church sign official papers. Harold Longenecker has rightly said: "Try by all means to make contact with some reputable attorney near your field of service. There will be many problems of a local nature that will be understood by your neighbourhood lawyer. He can help you around many difficult situations (44:62).

VIII. Miscellaneous Possibilities

Many new opportunities have opened in recent years. Developers for large shopping malls will give consideration for leasing space for an auditorium and Christian education rooms. This is especially so when you work with the developers while in the early planning stages of the shopping mall. This type of accomodation opens new avenues of ministry as you develop a church in the mall.

In a densely populated apartment area rooms were made available to a new church. In fact the superintendent was anxious for the church to serve his people.

Across North America there has been a trend to building residences for senior citizens with an attached auditorium and Christian education rooms.

Campus church sites have been built in a number of cities. This is where several denominations build under one roof. In some cases they share the same auditorium but stagger their services. In other situations they build two or three auditoriums but have common office area.

Evangelicals have been slow to enter campus church sites as we have a distinct message that could be compromised. There is likewise the problem of secondary separation. In fact, in a number of the campus church sites, the Sunday Schools are merged into one enterprise with teachers from various churches sharing the teaching positions. It would appear only a matter of time before the children raised in these churches lose sight of the distinctions of their own church.

There are some advantages in leasing space. You have no capital to invest. Off-street parking is provided. You have no buildings to maintain. You devote your whole ministry to people.

IX. What about Free Sites?

At times, well meaning people will offer you a site without cost or at a reduced price. Too many congregations have accepted such offers only to regret it later. Offers should be carefully considered and, if accepted, there should be no limitation as to their use. There should be the liberty to trade or sell for a more suitable site, if this is advisable.

X. Advanced Site Purchasing

A number of denominations are purchasing sites from two to five years before a church is started. This is what the Home Mission Board of the Fellowship Baptists is seeking to do. A number of choices sites have been secured. Each site will be made available to the local church upon its establishment for the total actual cost to the Fellowship. In this way, land is purchased before it has further appreciated in cost.

A fine 3.5 acre site was purchased in October, 1976, in Brandon, Manitoba. Seven months later the church came to the Fellowship and recommended a different corner. Within seven months the original site had appreciated $10,000. It is the policy of the Fellowship Baptists not to make money on land and thus the local church received a bonus of $10,000 for their new site.

There should be more planning on a long-range basis. Local municipal offices have projections and studies of future subdivisions. Although these are subject to change yet they can serve as a guideline. Pre-develop-land is much cheaper than land that is fully serviced.

Example of a Church Planter
Who knows How to Choose Sites

Church Planter Alex Rockwell is an excellent example of one who knows how to lead a new church in the purchase of property.

Grace Baptist Church, Charlottetown, Prince Edward Island, might well be called a miracle church. Four families met in June, 1973, and presented their case for the need of a new work in their city. Pastor and Mrs. Alex Rockwell were appointed by the Fellowship Baptist Home Mission Board and started their work in November, 1973. Within two years the congregation was running over 180 in the morning services. During this period of time over 75 made professions of faith and were baptized. Eleven young people were attending various schools of higher learning preparing for Christian service, before the church was four years old.

One of the interesting developments in this opening period ministry was the purchase of a large 25 acre site, with about 1,300 feet bordering on the Trans-Canada Highway. The church sold 15 acres for house sites, this gave them sufficient funds so that their 10 acres, including a choice corner lot, was then debt free.

Pastor Rockwell, in response to the question how he determined the size of the church lot, said: "We did this by determining what our program should be over a twenty-five year span. We estimated how large our church might be in that time and calculated that if it didn't turn out that way we could always sell unnecessary land. However, if our church grew and we did not have the property then we would have no choice, and land is going to be a lot more expensive in the future."

He was asked how he located such a fine site. "We were definately lead of the Lord to this church site. We had attempted to purchase two or three other sites which we considered good ones but always had our eye on this one. However, it seemed a hopeless dream. We made an offer on one site which was not accepted. At that time we learned that a member of our own congregation had the rights to the site which we have now purchased. The land had been "frozen" by the government because they were going to put an access route through to the Charlottetown bypass. As soon as this freeze was taken off the individual got the rights to the land and then, when he found out we had not yet purchased a site, gave it over to us. Many business people have since marvelled that we got this choice site."

This type of a situation means that someone must develop the housing sites. He answered the following question. Is it better for the church to develop the extra land into a subdivision or to turn it over to a private developer to do it? "This is a difficult question to answer and I suppose that the answer will vary with the local situation. In our case we found that developers want to have a large 'slice of the pie' and we would have simply been providing a vehicle for them to make money. We decided that God had allowed things to turn out this way so that our church site would be entirely paid for by the sale of the subdivision. This is the way it turned out."

Pastor Rockwell testifies that it really helps the morale of the congregation when land has been secured. When public buildings are being used the congregation feels that they are floating. Actual land purchase gives a feeling of solidity.

The church noticed a sharp increase in offerings once they had something into which to put their money. This is a pattern when churches step out by faith and purchase property.

Yes, property is an asset. It increases the stewardship of a congregation. It leads them to take a step of faith. It raises their morale. It is a testimony to the community as to the stability of the new church. And of course it adds to the financial assets of the church.

Chapter 15

Dovercourt Baptist Church
New Horizons Tower, Toronto, Ontario

FORM FOLLOWS FUNCTION

The Baptist pastor was proudly conducting an inspection tour of the new $300,000 educational building being completed by his church. The visitors were city officials, all Roman Catholics. "This is certainly a fine building", said one. Another asked how it would be used. After listing a brief resume of the usual activities — Sunday School, youth fellowship, prayer meeting and monthly socials — the enquirer shook his head sadly and remarked, "Too bad. Such fine facilities as these should be used more than a few hours each week. Is this a wise stewardship of God's money?"

At first impulse the pastor was insulted. He was now working twice the standard forty hours per week administering and ministering to a "busy church". It was open seven days a week. There was hardly a night but what at least one activity was scheduled, and some nights two or three. His own body aching with unrelieved weariness and many of the most faithful of the hard core of workers were seriously calling for relief. And now this "outsider" was saying, "You and your people are not working hard enough!" But that was NOT what he said. He said the building would not be working hard enough. This editorial taken from the "Watchman Examiner" strikes home to us who are engaged in building edifices.

I. Form Follows Functions

It is important to know what functions we plan to carry on in the building before we plan the form. One of the first steps is therefore to plan for the functions to be held in the building. The building is a tool for the church, and not the other way around. Too often congregations have tried to fit a ministry into a particular building. M. Wendell Belew suggests that "Church buildings in themselves are great assets, or liabilities. In some areas their ornate beauty attracts seekers; in other areas they repulse. Some church buildings have been designed for a type of program or a form of gathering which is no longer relevant. Some structures have become a fetish which has claimed its devotees and exploited them of their reason for being a church. (5:24)"

In the final analysis our ministry is people, not a building. The latter is only a tool — a vessel — of the congregation. This is why you cannot expect the building itself to draw a congregation. Many pastors and congregations labour under the wrong notion that when you put up a building the congregation will fill it. Church facilities will not necessary produce growth. Many excellent and adequate church buildings are half-filled today. It's the staff and the people with a ministering program that will produce growth and vitality in a local church. We need buildings providing we recognize the purpose for the same and plan ahead before we build.

II. Inflexible Space is Wasteful

Poor planning can result in wasted space. A pastor of a new church sat in my office and showed me plans for their first unit. The building was planned for 9600 square feet. He was asked two questions: what is the edifice going to cost and what is your annual income? He did not have the answer for the first question. Annual income amounted to $15,000. Within a matter of moments he was brought face to face with reality. He had no estimate of the actual cost of building today and was disappointed to hear that his planned structure would probably cost $310,000 to $340,000 to build. In addition, he had large rooms set apart for Sunday School departments. This space would be used twice a week, flexibility was not part of the plan for the use of the building. He was interested to observe how that same Sunday School space could be worked into additional use by making it part of the auditorium, by way of a folding door or window.

III. Take Time to Plan for a Total Ministry

Pastor Robert Daley who works for the Home Mission Board
of the Baptist General Conference urges building committees to
give sufficient time to planning. He says that "Church planning
and building always take longer than we would wish, so patience
is needed. We are sometimes tempted to think planning costs are
an additional cost that can be avoided by-and-large. Planning is
in reality the most essential part of building and will determine
the beauty, function, versatility, efficiency and maintainance
costs of your facility. Good plans are a valuable asset, as much a
part of the building as are the steel brick and fixtures. Any
lending institution will count good plans one of your most
valuable assets. (90:)

George Fletcher, a consultant with the Church Architecture
Department of the Baptist Sunday School Board, points out
three normal phases a church should go through in erecting a
building.

> The first is the survey phase, a time to evaluate what exists,
> what is happening, and what can and needs to be done in
> relation to church program and building. The second is the
> planning phase. This is the process of planning the building
> space to meet the needs discovered and determined in the
> survey. The third is the construction phase. This is the time
> when the construction prints are completed, contracts let,
> and the building constructed.
> When planning a building program these phases should
> always be followed in this sequence. If either phase is
> omitted or taken out of sequence, the results will be a
> building built, but not planned; needs will continue to exist
> that cannot be met, and money will have been wasted that
> should have been used wisely for God's Kingdom (88:32).

In your survey try to envision the next five to twenty-five years
of ministry of the church. This includes the possible services of a
day-care centre or home for senior citizens or a Christian day
school.

What kind of a site is needed to meet the needs discovered by
your survey? What kind of a community should you be located in
for your anticipated ministry? What kind of sheltered space will
you need? What style of building will best suit your future needs?

This type of survey will assist you in measuring the costs
against benefits. It will force you to distinguish between institutional self-glorification and a ministry to people.

Mind you, "it is not possible to construct a building which will serve for all time to come. Improvements, new ideas and new equipment will continually be introduced into church buildings. It will be necessary to think through the entire program as you plan the building. Many times it is necessary to construct one unit at a time. Even so, the complete and master plan should be adopted before any part of the building is started. (89:10) This is good counsel for your survey committee.

IV. The First Unit

It is reasonable to assume that a new church will not likely be in a position to build the ultimate edifice for a number of years. Most new churches plan to build in stages. Elmer Towns when interviewing the pastors of the ten largest Sunday Schools suggests that you never get out of a building program. This means that a congregation should always plan another building for added growth. "Christianity is a process not a product. Therefore the young congregation should always be building additional rooms or enlarging the auditorium. Physical expansion reflects spiritual growth and if a church is winning souls they will need more space to teach and preach. Also when the neighbourhood sees additions being built they realize the church is growing. (5:156)"

V. The Portable Unit

Many young congregations use a portable in the early period of growth. This gives the church a base for their operation. There is a psychological advantage in that a small group does not rattle around in a portable. This gives the congregation a financial goal to meet that, once paid off, is a stepping stone to your first permanent unit.

Portable units can be secured from schools selling a portable classroom. Certain house plans can be changed to meet the needs of a house church for a period of time. One firm in Toronto is now building relocatable buildings that are so designed they can be moved in sections. Each section is 12' x 36' and the materials meet urban codes for a permanent building.

VI. Functional Space

Another phase of the planning is to design space that is functional. Try to get away from the traditional concept of a church building. J. Daniel Baumann has well said: "What is required for the contemporary church building is not a fake or fictitious imitation of the past. For instance, gothic architecture was fine for the thirteenth century, but a church built in the 1970's should be an authentic and honest expression of the faith into the materials and forms of today." In the same line T. Lee Anderson adds:

Because of the high cost of property and construction today, buildings must be used to utmost efficiency. At the same time, churches are developing new types of programs and ministries which have new space requirements. This means the space must be planned for flexibility of use. If folding doors or removable wall panels are used, a department room may be subdivided into classrooms. It may also be combined with other department rooms into a fellowship hall, recreation area, or day care centre. It may also serve as overflow seating for the auditorium.

Today the rate of change in education, construction, technology, and standards of living is increasing rapidly. Buildings of new techniques, organization and equipment. Since the types and sizes of spaces needed are likely to change, the building should be designed so the interior partitions can be easily shifted or removed. These partitions should not support the roof or floor structure above. Instead, the structure should be supported on the exterior walls and / or columns and beams. Electrical, plumbing, heating and air conditioning systems should also be designed for flexibility and easy change. (3:143,144)

Careful planning will enable the congregation to erect a functional, flexible building. This will tend to reduce unusable space and at the same time reduce the overall construction costs as it may not need to be as large as first planned.

With the way the political climate is developing, churches might well be forced to reconsider the way they are using their facilities. Will our governments continue to give churches freedom to use their buildings in such a limited way? With so many social needs, with a serious lack of energy and limited land area that is serviced, we might be forced to change and provide a greater service to the community. Blessed is that congregation that has sought to keep in mind the needs of the area and builds accordingly.

VII. Design of the Auditorium

Consideration must be given to the interior of the auditorium. Here the New Testament concept of the priesthood of believers should be expressed.

It is encouraging to see more and more houses of worship

being designed from a basic circular pattern rather than a long rectangle. It is difficult for people to feel that they are gathered with a community of fellow servants, bringing their strengths and weaknesses before God, His Word, and a forgiving community if they are seated so that their primary view is the back of heads of others in the congregation. The same is the case if they view only the worship leaders. (54:57)

It is actually easier to communicate when the people are around you. A church auditorium designed in a semicircle can seat 350 people with only 8 or 9 rows of seats. Compare this with a rectangle auditorium which would perhaps need 18 to 20 pews.

The pulpit should be centrally located. This emphasizes the important role of the Bible in our services. Donald F. Ackland has well said: "A Central pulpit and an open Bible place the emphasis where it should be placed — upon the revealed Word which at once inspires our worship, declares our doctrines, authenticate our ordinances, sustains our spiritual vigor, and points the way of life to sinful man.

Provide adequate light as it will aid in worship. We are people of the Book and if that be so, we need to be able to read as the messages are outlined in the Word of God. I never could quite understand why in some fundamental churches the lights are dimmed just before the sermon.

Congregational singing is important in our churches. Special music by a choir or groups adds to the services. It is wise to develop a good accoustical setting to aid in this part of the ministry.

VIII. Plan the Use of the Pulpit Area

In my chapter of "Preach It, Brother" emphasis is placed on preaching for a decision. It's a meaningful experience for a person to step forward and express his desire to accept Jesus Christ, be baptized or to unite with the membership, or for that matter, to make some other decision. Plan the pulpit area with this in mind so that there is sufficient room.

Most Christian couples desire a church setting for their wedding. Funeral services for members are often held in the church building. For these future occasions your building committee should plan accordingly.

IX. Pews or Chairs?

Although pews are used traditionally for a church auditorium, actually chairs are much more flexible and make the space functional. There are a number of styles on the market today that are both comfortable and aesthetic.

X. Provide for the Physically Handicapped

More innovations are being enforced today in the public buildings to care for the physically handicapped. Motels and hotels now have certain standards to care for these special needs. And this is a good thing! Physically handicapped people will soon know if you care for them by the way you provide for their needs. It is wise to eliminate exterior steps as far as possible, or at least have them enclosed. Wide entrances into rooms and spacious corridors with suitable hand rails will greatly assist those who need to use a wheel chair. The hard of hearing should also be given consideration. Do not over look the wash rooms in your structure.

XI. Is an Architect Needed?

An architect is needed to plan for the best use of the site you are developing. His training and talent will give you a better building. His fee is compensated by the services rendered and the money saved by suggesting new materials and construction techniques. A Christian architect who understands our ministries can best serve the church. Ask for the details of fees, and when and how payment will be due. J. Patrick Mitchell, who is a Christian architect suggests:

> *A competent architect can assist you to succeed in achieving immediate and long range expansion goals. Expansion goals in terms of brick and wood are a means to an end, the end being souls won for Christ. Therefore, your goals being to reach all the lost in your community, you will need to employ all known successful methods to accomplish the task. The Lord has given each one a talent and He admonishes us to invest and use it wisely. The architect has a special talent and can help far more than some realize. (106)*

XII. Tax Rebate

There are some areas in North America where the provincial or state capital will give a rebate on the sales tax paid for building materials, church furnishings and Sunday School equipment. In fact, many items are covered in this ruling. You will want to consult your own taxation office.

An example is the Province of Ontario where the sales tax rebate is based on the total contract cost. It is important that you keep a strict account of all bills paid for materials, labour, and subcontractors. This will help expedite your rebate. For further information in Ontario write Queens Park, Toronto, and ask for Retail Sales Tax Regulation 785 dealing with rebates.

It was my privilege to pastor Dovercourt Baptist Church, Toronto, at the time we launched forth in a new $2,200,000 building that would house a church auditorium, Christian education space and a residence for senior citizens. Our sales tax rebate amounted to $63,734.

Example of a Church Planter Who built a Functional Building.

Brian J. Baxter commenced his work as a church planter at the West Highland Baptist Church, Hamilton, Ontario, in February, 1973. The group had their first meeting in October, 1972, with the desire to form a new work on the Hamilton mountain. There were 50 meeting at the time of the coming of Pastor Baxter and offerings were about $235 a week. Four years later, at the completion of a new building, the attendance was just under 200 with weekly offerings exceeding $1200.

Besides being a keen Bible teacher, the Lord has given Brian Baxter an understanding of flexible and functional space. Having just formed a new church, funds were limited. Yet, with a growing congregation steps had to be taken to house the church.

One of the first steps was to determine their ultimate objective as a congregation. In their judgment they set a goal of a 500 maximum — the decision being partly based on the size of property they were able to secure. Actually this church had to pay $70,000 for a 1.5 acre site. The next step was to plan to build for half their projected growth in the first unit.

The church faced three options:

1. To have an architect and a contractor would mean hiring an architect to design the building and put it out for tender and hire a contractor to build it.

2. To have an architect — superintendent — This method was to hire an architect as shown in number 1. above. When plans were ready, the building committee would act as contractor, hire a superintendent of construction, and hire all the subcontractors but supervise the construction.

3. Design-building — This method involves hiring a construction company who provide their own architect who designs the building with the committee and then the company constructs the edifice. The church adopted the last of the three options and had estimates and presentations from three firms

which operate this way.

One of the toughest questions faced by the congregation was how much to spend on the building. The church did not want to over-extend their financial commitment. On the other hand the church wanted to build a large edifice to meet their present needs.

Stress was laid on both flexible and functional space. By flexible space the thought was to have space to meet the maximum need but can still be divided to provide smaller units of space. Functional space is space that works. The church came up with a design that serves a multi-functional concept. The same area is used for many functions. This reduced the maximum edifice that normally would have been required for a congregation the size of West Highland.

Chairs are a necessity if the space is to be multifunctional. There are some disadvantages to chairs in that they take up slightly more space and they are noisy on tile. It is advisable to use wall to wall carpet when you use chairs. Although they have to be constantly straigthened. However, the advantages of economy, flexibility and comfort outweigh the disadvantages.

In response to the question: What suggestions would you give a pastor facing a building program he gave the following six suggestions:

1. Start to plan early
2. Don't rush into decisions.
3. Check your decision with other pastors and churches.
4. Check all final drawings to make sure you are getting exactly what you expect.
5. Prepare your people well. Keep them informed by progress reports both verbal and written.
6. Take care not to neglect the spiritual priority of your ministry during the building period.

In the total plan of the edifice: "Form follows function". Know what you want to do with space, and build accordingly. Remember, the building was made for the church, not the church for the building.

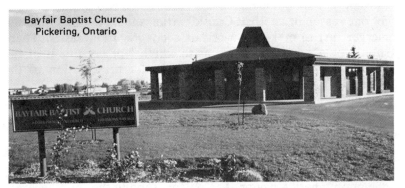

Chapter 16

Bayfair Baptist Church
Pickering, Ontario

TWO CAN LIVE AS
CHEAPLY AS ONE

"Two can live as cheaply as one" when it comes to the merger of two smaller churches in a community. In most cases, the advantages far outweigh the negative aspects.

One advantage is a lower financial budget. You have one pastors' remuneration and one building to maintain. An enlarged congregation can offer a more diversified ministry. Furthermore, youth, at least to a certain extent, are attracted by numbers. It is hard to get excited about a church service if you have only two or three your own age. Combining two congregations will perhaps greatly add to your youth attendance. Another advantage is the opportunity to unite the best talent and skills of the two churches. Selling the two original buildings will enable the merged congregation to erect a functional, flexible edifice.

While many believe churches should never close and merge, in reality, it can be beneficial, under certain circumstances. It is wise to consider such a move, when after a period of several years, neither church has made a spiritual dent in the community. A merger is advisable when neither church has proper facilities to carry on the work that is needed. Another reason for merger is when neither church is in a position to adequately look after the remuneration of a pastor. There have been times when two churches are too close together. In such an event, combining forces might well be for the best for the churches.

A merger should not take place just to get out from under a burden, nor should it take place because the two pastors want it for one reason or another. Consideration should not be given to a merger just to make the work of a congregation easier. There should be a genuine concern as to whether or not this is of the Lord. Can a merger bring about a better presentation of the gospel to the community?

What are some of the problems faced by merging churches?

I. Who Will be the Pastor?

This is one of the first problems to face, if both churches have a pastor at the time of the merger talks, or even if there is only one church with a pastor. The pastors serving the churches were called by the congregations to serve for an indefinite period of time. Is their ministry over, once a merger takes place? One solution to this is to carry on the merger when the pulpits are vacant. If however, there are pastors serving at the time of merger, there are three alternatives.

1. Both pastors are called to serve as co-pastors. This remains as such until one pastor leaves at a later date. The next pastor who comes will be an associate pastor. Co-pastors can present problems as to who will preach and when, who will have the marriages, burials, and who will have the final say. These guidelines should be drawn up before such a merger takes place if both pastors are to remain to serve the merged congregation.

2. One pastor resigns and the other pastor is called by the merged church. The only question here is to decide which pastor is going to move on. Furthermore, there are times when a pasotr might show favoritism to his former members, or former members might show the same to their pastor.

3. Both pastors resign and leave the community. This enables the merged church to call a new pastor. This is often the best as it gives the church an opportunity to seek fresh leadership for an anticipated expanding ministry.

II. Who will be the Members?

Some merging churches go through the experience of having the deacons of one church interview the members of the other. Most churches, however, accept the present membership and refer to that group as charter members. There is a problem as to how to handle inactive members. This must be settled on an individual base. A compromise would be to write such members and inform them of the proposed merger and to ask if they desire to join the new church.

III. Who will serve as Officers?

It has been a happy experience for a number of churches to use the deacons of the merging churches for the first year. In this way the two congregations get to know the deacons and can better determine at the annual business meeting those who should be called to continue to serve. Other official positions are generally settled in a mutually agreed manner. Many times one officer will resign to give the other officer the position. It is best to use officers from the two congregations so that each church senses a vital part of the new body.

IV. What about the Buildings?

This is a relative question depending on the local circumstances. The following questions will need to be faced by the merged congregation: Are either of the buildings suitable? Are either of the sites satisfactory? Is it better to sell both and erect a new one on one of the present sites? Is it better to sell both and relocate? In most cases, the merged church will find a new location and erect a modern edifice to meet the anticipated growth.

Once in a while there are circumstances where external conditions force one church to merge with another. This was the case of Langstaff Baptist Church, Thornhill, Ontario, when a new highway was built and changed the community. The church merged with Willowdale Baptist Church and sold the Langstaff building to the Department of Highways.

V. Are the Two Congregations Compatible?

Each church, like each individual, has its own personality and temperament. Not every congregation can yield a little in order to work a functioning merger. Two strong churches in one of our Canadian cities were giving serious consideration to uniting forces in order to build a super church, that in their judgment would better minister to the whole city. Everything went well until the final aspect when it was discovered that the churches differed a little on their emphasis on secondary separation. The vote was lost, not because the merger was not a good move, but because of the internal climate.

VI. What about the Statement of Faith and Constitution?

This can open up many problems that are really not necessary. If both churches belong to the same denominational affiliation, why not accept the official statement of faith of the national body? Most national bodies offer a sample constitution for a local church, which could be easily adapted to meet the needs of the new church.

Example of a successful Merger

One recent merger which has been most successful is that which brought Bay Ridges and Dunfair Baptist Churches to form what is today the Bayfair Baptist Church of Pickering, Ontario. The successful merger took place under the guidance of two pastors, Jack Hannah and Roy Vanderlip. As the merger was nearing completion, both pastors resigned. Later, Jack Hannah was called to serve as pastor, and continued as such, until he accepted the position as Secretary of the Church Ministries Board of the Fellowship of Evangelical Baptist Churches in Canada. Much credit for the successful merger should go to Pastor Vanderlip. His co-operative selfless spirit paved the way for negotiations.

The two churches were too closely situated to carry on an effective witness without hindering the other. Both churches, located on opposite sides of Frenchmen's Bay, were even closer when the highway department put through a road connecting the two sides of the bay.

Neither church had proper facilities for carrying on a self-supporting church. The Bay Ridges building was a portable structure, 24' x 48' with no basement or other building nearby for additional space. This presented a problem for an expanding church of the future.

Jack Hannah commenced his ministry in April, 1969. At the service there were five adults and four children. By December, after intensive visitation, the attendances were hitting the low 80's. How do you hold a Sunday School in a small building? It was partly resolved by one of the members driving his camper each week and parking it by the portable. This was used by the adult Bible class. As a matter of fact there was a real scramble into that camper because that was actually the warmest place. The portable was heated by oil and did not operate properly. Often the children would be singing in Sunday School and you could see their breath! In fact, many action choruses were sung just to keep warm.

The Dunfair Baptist Church building was just as limited. It was an old insul-brick structure that was first of all constructed on the corner of an old street. The church next put in a basement. Everything was done in a haphazard manner and it was most unattractive. There was a definite contrast between the church and the new homes springing up around it. The church building was just out-of-place. Their morning attendance was running around the 20 mark. There was a general spirit of defeat. The church was isolated — a forlorn building in the heart of an expanding community.

This was a perfect setting for discussions on the question of merger. Both congregations could see the advantage of combining forces and seeking to do a better job in communicating the gospel to their community. Both churches sensed the leading of the Lord. Both pastors were in full agreement. Thus it was early in 1970 that the foundation was laid which ultimately led to a successful merger. The Bay Ridge Church was packed out under the leadership of Jack Hannah. The church owned four building lots and had a small debt. After Bay Ridges sought Fellowship affiliation it became a natural thing for the two churches to merge as one strong work. The two pastors fostered the merger movement by encouraging joint evening services. This provided a sense of companionship and a fellowship that developed into the actual merger.

In the late spring of 1970 and through the summer, the deacons of the two churches met together and independently to work out various steps with regard to amalgamation. It was discovered that their statement of faith and constitutions were similar and thus did not pose any problem. It was agreed that the membership of both churches would come together to form the charter membership for the new church.

The idea was written in the amalgamation agreement that as soon as possible in the foreseeable future the church would move towards a new building. During the transition period the portable building of Bay Ridges was moved next to the Dunfair edifice. Jack Hannah cautions churches considering mergers to have a clear understanding about buildings. He went on to add: "Although we say we are not traditionalists we are very much tied to our old buildings and locations. This is a sensitive factor for those in leadership to look at with caution."

There really was no major problem in the merger except for the temperment of the congregations. The Bay Ridges members had really seen growth in the past year and the church was quite optimistic about the future and anxious to get going. Whereas the Dunfair members had not seen similar growth and therefore were planning for a drop in membership and a lower income. Bringing two congregations of different temperment together meant they had to be harnessed in order to get them to pull together. That meant putting a few brakes on the Bay Ridges members on account of their optimism and their tendency to prod a few of the Dunfair members to get them moving a bit. Soon they saw fulfilled the old adage that a team of horses pulling together do not have time to kick one another.

In this type of merger there really was no disadvantage. However, there were several real advantages. There was a new spirit in the meetings due to an immediate larger congregation which brought optimism. It provided financial economy. With one pastor's remuneration the church could start saving for their new edifice. In addition, the four lots were sold to make the new work debt free, and at the same time made possible the purchase of a choice site between the major highways in Southern Ontario, 401 and number 2.

In 1969 the combined income of the two churches was under $6,000. The merged church has since erected a new quarter million dollar edifice. Offerings have increased almost year by year: 1971 — $16,000; 1972 — $24,000; 1973 — $36,000; 1974 — $47,000; 1975 — $75,000; 1976 — $72,000; 1977 — $85,000. This financial growth would probably not have been realized as quickly without the merger of the two churches.

Jack Hannah would caution leaders engaged in mergers to study the compatibility of the two congregations. Give thought as to how and where the constitutions differ. What about the schedule of services. What ministry is to be offered to the youth? Is it going to be Christian Service Brigade or Sky Force? Will there be a problem over the Sunday School curriculum? Will growth mean less personal attention? Are the two congregations prepared to assume the missionary commitments made previously by the two churches? Another area to work out relates to memorial gifts or furnishings from one or both of the churches.

Yes, two churches can live together as cheaply as one. In most cases the advantages for merger far outweigh the disadvantages if the conditions and circumstances are right.

Chapter 17

BURNING THE MIDNIGHT OIL

If ever a man burns the midnight oil, it's the bi-vocational pastor. During the week he is busy making a living for his family. Evenings and on Sundays he is engaged in a pastoral ministry. Such an individual, to be successful, knows how to separate the essentials from the non-essentials and to establish priorities in his schedule. He is usually highly motivated and has full confidence in delegating tasks to others.

Paul, the Apostle, was a bi-vocational pastor according to Acts 18:3. By occupation he made tents. In this way he was not a burden to the young churches financially.

Evangelical churches today owe much to a large group of pastors who are bi-vocational. Many of the churches had their start with a pastor who was willing to hold a secular position and still minister the Word of God. Judy Touchton, commenting on these pastors suggests: "From Paul to today, bi-vocational pastors — the 'tentmaking preachers' — have filled church history. They are the worker-priests, the non-stipendary clergy — the 'working preachers'. (88:5)"

I. Their Problems and Frustrations

1. Family life is different. The bi-vocational pastor does not have the same amount of time to spend with his family. Working

a minimum of from 35 to 40 hours a week, he just does not have the evenings or Saturdays available for family activities. Of necessity, the evenings must be spent in study and visitation work. Sundays and certain evenings will be filled with services and committee meetings. This reduces the amount of time he is going to have with his family. However, such an individual can compensate by making the time he has with his family most profitable. It is not the amount of time parents spend with their children, rather, the quality of their experiences together. For example, an unbelieving drunken husband has little to offer his family while intoxicated. In a family where there is considerable quarreling, the time together can be a negative factor. One can readily see that a Godly bi-vocational pastor can make the most of his family time and actually accomplish more than many other fathers.

2. There is seldom enough time for thorough sermon preparation. While most pastors are busy in their study during the morning hours, the bi-vocational pastor is busy working. He must squeeze his study time in during the evenings and perhaps lunch hours. As a result there is not always the depth and variety that a congregation might expect. One way to meet this problem is to have a reduced number of services. Often a congregation expects the bi-vocational pastor to have the full range of activities of the average church: Sunday School, morning and evening services, midweek prayer hour, youth groups and visitation. While it is commendable to have a full schedule, it is really expecting too much of a bi-vocational pastor. He just cannot minister effectively with such a weekly schedule. Another way to compensate is to turn over a number of the messages and Bible studies to gifted laymen. This is in keeping with Ephesians chapter four in developing the gifts of believers.

3. A bi-vocational pastor misses many of the associational meetings of fellow pastors as well as some of his denominational sessions. Most of these functions are held during the day when he is secularly employed. At the same time denominational sessions are held in different cities where he is unable to attend. This is a serious handicap because a pastor needs the fellowship of other pastors. The spiritual reinforcement of sharing together is important. The problem could be resolved to a certain extent if more sessions were held in the evenings or on Saturday.

4. The bi-vocational pastor does not always have the academic and theological education of his peers. There are some that do. Bi-vocational pastor Adrian Crewson of the Baptist Church of the Open Bible in Windsor, Ontario. while a student at Central

Baptist Seminary, Toronto, earned high honours in Bible, Greek and Hebrew. However, this is the exception rather than the rule. This can be somewhat compensated for by taking available course through Theological Education by Extension. A number of Bible colleges and seminaries operate with a variety of courses suitable for a bi-vocational pastor through correspondence.

It should be kept in mind that, while the bi-vocational pastor may lack theological education, he does have experience in his own work that can be an asset. Many times these same pastors can balance the budget and finances much better than the average full time pastor.

5. It can be detrimental to a church not to have a part in the remuneration of a pastor. There is not the same motivation to support the local church, when you have a "free" pastor. This is where the bi-vocational pastor will seek to prepare his church for the day when a pastor will be supported. It takes real grace to resign from a church when this point is reached.

II. Advantages of a Bi-Vocational Pastor

1. These pastors have an inside contact with the secular world. Yes, on Sundays, they are pastors, but during the week, they are fellow teachers, salesmen, accountants or may be involved in other occupations. They have an opportunity to rub shoulder to shoulder with people the average salaried pastor does not have. This identification with fellow workers can lead to a natural witnessing situation. There is an attitude on the part of the community that a pastor is paid to witness. This is not so with the bi-vocational pastor as there is not the same gap to be bridged.

2. A bi-vocational pastor can open the doors of a new church. This is especially so in areas that are often missed by a denomination due to the size of the community. In opening a new work the major part of the cost of the first year is not the building but the pastor's remuneration. You can appreciate that, if this is covered, many new doors will readily open to a gospel church.

3. A bi-vocational pastor tends to have a practical pulpit ministry. Being in the secular world throughout the week he is able to identify with the problems and minister to them. His ministry is not theoretical but practical. It is a down to earth approach seeking to meet the needs of men and to minister the Word to seeking hearts. People are hurting today and the bi-vocational

III. Ways to Help Bi-Vocational Pastors

1. Assistance might be given in locating fields where new churches are needed. Most denominational offices know of areas where there are opportunities for starting new churches. The Home Mission Board of the Fellowship of Evangelical Baptist Churches in Canada has over one hundred towns and cities where new churches could start immediately. Manpower and financial resources are lacking. Bi-vocational pastors may well be the key for future expansion in North America!

2. Financial help could be made available for assisting with moving expenses. This is a legitimate use of home mission offerings. Further, it serves to encourage bi-vocational pastors to relocate in needy areas.

3. Financial help might be needed in the opening months until the pastor is well established with his secular employment. This is especially so for a business man who has a clientele to build up for a livelihood.

4. Cassettes and papers along with good books might be furnished to assist with additional training. An experienced pastor might well serve as a guide to specific courses of study.

5. Periodic visits by fellow pastors and denominational leaders will encourage and lift his morale.

IV. What is the Future for Bi-Vocational Pastors?

Their numbers of necessity will have to increase. If new churches are going to open as they are needed today, more men will have to respond to this work. Lyly Schaller, a church growth specialist, predicts that by 1985 half of the ministers in the United States will be bi-vocational. (88:5) The Fellowship Baptist Home Mission Board, sensing the need for new churches, and recognizing that funds will not permit salaried pastors to fill all open doors, are working with Theological Education by Extension courses. The goal is to train and equip men to serve as bi-vocational pastors. The foundation was laid by the French Board of the Fellowship of Evangelical Baptist Churches in Canada under their Secretary, Rev. William L. Phillips. He saw the need to train the French youth to reach the Province of Quebec. This resulted in the preparation of seven courses for their own Theological Education by Extension ministry. Their present enrollment exceeds one hundred and ten young men. Thus dozens of French youth are now being trained, by extension, to open up many of the unevangelized towns and cities of Quebec. There are great opportunities to establish churches in towns and cities where there are thousands of people without a gospel church.

It is anticipated with the combined efforts of the Fellowship French and Home Boards the number of Fellowship Churches in Canada could double in the 1980's. Can one visualize the potential if all the evangelical churches of different denominations got involved in such a ministry?

V. Example of one Bi-Vocational Pastor

One bi-vocational pastor, now in his third church, is Ted Clark of Vermilion Baptist Church, Vermilion, Alberta. Ted believes God has uniquely called and trained him for this ministry.

He studied for the pastorate at the Northwest Baptist Theological College and Seminary, Vancouver, British Columbia. In addition he is a professional Chartered Accountant. In regards to the work of a bi-vocational pastor he suggests that certain vocations do not lend themselves well to this dual ministry as they demand too much effort and the work of the Lord will suffer. The professional fields such as accounting and teaching are ideal. Likewise, self-employed people who can regulate their hours, can more easily take on this type of challenge. Certain occupations such as travelling salesmen would present a problem because of the time spent away from the community and work.

In connection with this ministry, Ted claims that the most serious problem is that of time. He claims you are obligated to give service to your employer, your family and your church. All must fit into a busy schedule. He proceeds to talk about the lack of time for such important things as visitation and adequate time for sermon preparation. He gives his testimony that it is amazing how God gives extra grace and insight. At times the message gets across better than usual in spite of the pastor, he says.

Ted claims that it is much easier to relate to people in the market place and in the business world as a bi-vocational pastor. In fact, there are probably few tensions between pastor and people when a church has a bi-vocational pastor.

One of the joys Ted has experienced is the participation of his family in the churches. Family discussions are held to determine how and where each member may have a part. The witness and consistent testimony has helped to bring others into the churches.

Ted gave a resounding *yes* in response to the question relating to whether or not there was a need for additional bi-vocational pastors. He thinks this is part of the answer to the expansion of new churches. He regrets the fact that mission boards are forever writing about their shortage of funds. It is not that he is opposed to missions and church planters. He claims there is a limit to the available financial resources of our churches. With it costing about $1,300.00 as a minimum to support a married man and family each month, he questions how many new churches can be started in a year, realizing that it takes three to five years before the grant is removed.

Mission boards must recognize that many churches are stretched to the limit. It is possible that if more bi-vocational pastors enter the field, consideration should be given to assist new churches with gifts for land purchasing. Perhaps money could be made available to help with the cost of construction of an edifice.

It should be understood that it takes longer for a church with a bi-vocational pastor to become self-supporting. However, the funds that normally would have been given to a field with a bi-vocational pastor can be placed in a field with a salaried church planter. Thus you have two new churches at the financial cost of one!

Ted concludes his remarks by adding that the life of a bi-vocational pastor is not soft and easy. Many times one would like to say, "I'm going to take the day off but along comes a call and off you go to visit and help someone in need".

From my perspective, bi-vocational pastors are not second-rate ministers. If anything, these men are unusual in that they have been called to fulfill two roles, to live two lives and to speak in two ways. Bi-vocational pastors are part of the answer to the great anticipated expansion of the eighties.

Chapter 18

Forest Hills Fellowship Baptist Church
Dartmouth, N.S.

A PASTOR NEEDS A HOME TOO

$\mathbf{T}$he practice of many churches has been to provide a house, commonly called a parsonage, for their pastor and his family. There is, however, a marked trend away from this today, for reasons that will be discussed later in this chapter. Starting a new church affords an opportunity to break with this traditional aspect of church policy, establishing in its place, the policy of personal home ownership. Note some of the advantages of a pastor owning his own home.

I. Buys one to Further his Ministry

The very nature of a new work entails, at least for a time, the use of the pastor's home as a public meeting place. He will therefore, choose a house that is strategically located and condusive to group meetings without interfering with his family's living space or privacy. He may, as many pastors have done, purchase a house with a walk-in basement. This part of the house can be used as a chapel for prayer meetings and other activities. In house-hunting with one church planter, we came across a large house with two front entrances. One led into the main hallway and the second to a side room which could be a study and office. In this way people would be able to visit the pastor without having to go through the parsonage.

II. Buys one to fit Needs of his Family

The members of a church are at a great disadvantage when they try to provide adequate housing for their future pastors. One pastor might have five children and the next only one. One pastor might have his aged parents living with him, while another might not be married.

III. Provides Natural Family Living

The pastor, in his own home, is free to be himself. He and his wife can remodel or redecorate their home according to their own likes without having to seek the approval of the church. In a parsonage, on the other hand, the pastor's loyalties are divided. One pastor, for example, having resigned from the church, left behind the drapes along with several other items. The church members were quick to point out to their new pastor these evidences of their former pastor's liberality. Consequently, he felt obligated to leave the drapes in place, for a time, even though they did not fit in with their furnishing or tastes in decorating. This type of mental struggle can be avoided when the pastor is free to choose his own home.

IV. No Work for the Congregation

One real advantage for both the pastor and the church of personal home ownership is that the church is not responsible for the upkeep of the pastor's home. Most churches will redecorate the parsonage only when a new pastor has been called. The upkeep of the parsonage tends to be neglected in the case of a pastor who has served the church faithfully for many years. It is sad that it takes a change in pastoral leadership before the church will agree to renovate the parsonage!

Changing the wallpaper in a room or the color of the kitchen is therapy for the pastor's wife. In a parsonage, however, this type of expenditure has to be approved by the church, this, the expression of her personality in her home tends to be restricted.

The provision of a parsonage tends to be a rather impersonal business arrangement between the pastor and the church. The pastor's sense of responsibility for the upkeep of his home is displaced by the church's rules and regulations to this effect. At times I have noted the paint peeling on a parsonage and the grass tall and weedy around the house. Home ownership can provide the freedom and the incentive for the pastor to care for the appearance of his home.

V. Provides for a Longer Pastorate.

Home ownership can result in a longer pastorate and provide for a more stable ministry. For example, it is my understanding that the average length of a pastorate in the Southern Baptist Convention is three and a half years. It would be interesting to compare the length of service of pastors housed in parsonages with that of pastors who are home owners.

VI. Provides for his Retirement

Consider the advantages of home ownership upon retirement. Many pastors have little financial security to show for their long years of service and so are forced to let their children and the government support them when they reach retirement age. Others, of necessity, have really had to lower their standard of living, spending their crowning years in conditions next to poverty.

One pastor was called to a church in 1952. A lovely house was purchased as a parsonage for $15,000. The pastor served the church well having a fruitful and happy ministry. Upon his retirement in 1976 the parsonage was valued at $65,000. There was no way the retiring pastor could purchase a house of that value. Yet he did not profit from the rate of inflation and the church kept the prize for herself. If a church profits from this type of property appreciation, surely there is a moral obligation to share part of it with the man of God who has faithfully served that community for so many years! Home ownership avoids this problem.

VII. Home Ownership can help the Church

In some instances it has been to the advantage of a church financially to provide an allowance for the pastor so that he may own his own home. One church was approaching a major building program. The church offered their pastor the option of selling the parsonage and adding an amount to his remuneration so as to purchase his own house. The large cash sum from the parsonage could then be applied to the erection of the new church edifice. This enabled the congregation to add a larger Christian Education wing which resulted in an expended ministry. The latter increased the weekly offerings which in turn handled the extra living allowance of the pastor.

VIII. Consider the Tax Advantages

One must consider the tax advantages of home ownership. The equivalent to what is a reasonable rental value may be deducted as a tax exemption. Furthermore, in the United States one deducts interest paid on a house mortgage. In Canada, one does not pay a capital gain tax on the appreciation of a house when it is sold.

IX. Times when Home Ownership is not Wise

This would perhaps be so in a rural area where the demand for housing is more limited. This would apply to an inner city area where usually large houses are available and financially out of reach for the average pastor.

Another disadvantage is present if the pastor has to live out of the congregation's community. This reduces his visitation ministry, increases his auto expenses and consumes valuable time in running back and forth from his home to his field of service.

The pastor needs to be aware that in a depressed market he might lose financially on his house. It is a relative thing, although in recent years real estate has been a good investment.

William J. Hanson comments on a way the congregation might assist a pastor who owns his own home and is moving to assume a new responsibility:

> One thing should be mentioned about protecting the congregation and the pastor from liability to sell a pastor-owned residence when the pastor is ready to leave. Some pastors and congregations have entered into covenants where the congregation agrees to purchase the pastor's residence if it is not sold by the time the pastor is to leave. This is usually done on the basis of an appraised value. The congregation can then sell the home to the next pastor if he desires it, keep it as income property, or dispose of it on the open market. (80.4)

X. How to Purchase a House

If you decide to have a church-owned parsonage, have it several blocks away from your church site. A parsonage next door to the church building encroaches upon the privacy of the pastor and his family. Jack R. Bagwell has rightly said:

> The pastorium should not be located adjacent to existing church buildings.

1. The pastor is in a 'fish bowl'.
2. He is expected to attend all meetings at the church no matter how unrelated to his task. (He's home, his car's in the drive.)
3. He becomes the church janitor, turning off all lights, locking doors etc. (90:108)

Purchasing your own house will enable you to locate several blocks from your church site, if you have one, or within the community in which you are planning to work. One pastor lived forty miles from his church site. It was long-distance for families to telephone him. It is no wonder his ministry lasted less than two years. In these days of high fuel costs it is wise to be able to live near enough so as not to be obligated to drive you car to the church building or take public transit. Be sure, however, to be far enough away from the church to provide privacy for your family.

In beginning a work, try to secure a house large enough to hold some church functions. There are some advantages in using a home for mid-week and smaller services. A home creates a warm atmosphere. People are less formal and feel more at ease. Usually there is a friendly spirit that one does not always experience in a school gymnasium. The easy chairs of a home make it more comfortable and, if there is a fireplace, an extra dimension is added to the atmosphere.

There is a negative aspect to a home setting. Some folks will not come to a private home. They do not represent a high percentage, yet this factor must be kept in mind. This is especially true of Sunday services. It is better to have Sunday services in a neutral place and to keep homes for smaller week-night meetings.

Get to know the real value of houses before you offer to purchase one. A successful realtor has given two pieces of advice. One is that real estate in North America is a fairly sound investment in an age where other securities are uncertain. The second is, before buying a house, look at twenty-five or more. By that time you will know the market and be in a better position to make a wise decision.

You need to watch the salesman's line: "This house won't last long on the market". That could be so . . . but there will always be another bargain!

Example of Church Planter
Who knew How to Buy a House

Church planter Clair Hofstetter moved to Dartmouth, Nova

Scotia, in 1971. Two families started what is today the Forest Hills Baptist Church, now meeting in a beautiful new structure. Pastor Hofstetter settled on the community where the church was to be located. Next he purchased a home with a walk-in finished basement, which served the church for many months. Being a bachelor at the time, he was able to use one bedroom as the church nursery. He used another bedroom for a study. His living room and kitchen were excellent for Sunday School space.

He was able to develop a fine rapport with his neighbours. As a result, there were no serious complaints when he set up a sign announcing services. He saw to it that his people did not block the driveways of the residences on the block.

When he married, he had a home for his bride.

In six years the real estate value of his house has appreciated 80%. It is still appreciating due to the many housing developments in the community.

In response to my question, what are the advantages of home ownership, Pastor Hofstetter said:

The pastor who owns a home is building up a personal equity that he often does not do otherwise. Those monthly mortgage payments are a disciplined way of investing. The appreciation of value of real estate over the past six years has resulted in the doubling of one's investment. There is no real evidence that this will not continue to happen in the years to come, given present inflationary rates. A home is a solid investment. The ownership of a home brings an added stability to a pastor's ministry. The congregation realizes that he is not as likely to be a 'here today — gone tomorrow' type of pastor. For a home mission pastor it adds credibility to the community that he has come to their area to start a church and intends to see it through. The pastor himself will be less prone to 'Monday-morning' resignations with the sobering realization that he has a personal investment of which he would have to dispose.

The pastor who is a handy man will always have an outlet on those days off — fixing here, adding something there, renovating this, redecorating that, without ever having to consult a trustees' board, or wonder what one of the deacon's wives will say. It's his own home.

This will be an immense relief also to the pastor's wife when she has a notion to redecorate. Pastors who have families will experience less friction when Franky or Willie knocks over a newly planted tree, or breaks a post in the fence, or dents the aluminum siding with a misdirected stone. The reduction in friction between the pastor's family and the trustees' board over the parsonage, its upkeep and the wear and tear on it can be a real relief.

As a family you will be free to entertain when you want to; have friends and relatives stay overnight as often as you wish without feeling that you need to explain.

There is an added sense of privacy with home ownership versus parsonage living. The congregation will not decide that they have the right to use your home for whatever function they may plan as they sometimes do when they own the parsonage in which you live.

Home ownership also gives the pastor a closer identification with his families who own their own homes or are entering into home ownership and have the burden of a mortgage and what that means in terms of the monthly budget.

Pastor Hofstetter is able to see the other side as well. He gives the following disadvantages of home ownership:

There is the expense and work of upkeep during times when the pastor is extremely busy in the Lord's work. There is the temptation to care for the leaking faucet or the loose cupboard door instead of the lost soul or the lonely invalid. There is the anxiety and cost involved in resale if one should for some reason have a short pastorate. The high cost of housing in some metropolitan areas for a young pastor who hasn't even a downpayment would make home ownership an impossibility.

In the case of Pastor Hofstetter, home ownership assisted in starting the new church. School rent was very high, approaching $100 a day. The house chapel would seat 85 thus providing ample room for a new work. The home was a convenient place for back yard Bible clubs, prayer meetings, youth gatherings and other church functions. The home was much more accessible to the community than an apartment would have been. It provided rooms for counsel and made it possible to offer hospitality. Many times refreshments were served after the Sunday services. People enjoyed this time of fellowship.

Now, six years later, the members of this church are happy to be in their new edifice valued at about $200,000. It is a growing congregation as a result of faithful ministry on the part of pastor and people.

One Sunday in February, 1977, I was ministering in this church. On the way to Sunday School, the pastor took a different direction in order to pick up five new children he had discovered in his door-to-door visitation during the previous week. Next he will work on the parents. And so the church grows!

Yes, "A Pastor Needs a Home Too". In the case of Pastor Hofstetter his house was a stepping stone in the establishment of the Forest Hills Baptist Church, Dartmouth, Nova Scotia.

Chapter 19

CAN THESE BONES LIVE AGAIN

"**C**an these bones live again?" (Exel.37:3) might well be asked of churches in crisis and transition. In fact, this is an ongoing question in many churches that are about ready to close their doors but, in seeking to hold on, are trying to justify their existence. By way of clarification, a church may be said to be in a crisis situation when its current programs of outreach and ministry are no longer effective in reaching and nurturing people for Christ, or when its members have not learned to adapt traditional programs to meet their needs or develop new programs.

I. Things that bring about a Church Crisis

A number of factors may bring a crisis situation to a church. Internal unrest and a breakdown in communication between leaders can have a serious impact on the church. The slogan: "United we stand, divided we fall," can be rightly applied to a local church. Many people do not desire to be part of a church where, over a long period of time, issues are unresolved and where there is a constant spirit of unrest and bickering. Peaceful people will gradually slip away to a more peaceful congregation or simply cease attending any church. Dr. Hollis Green states:

As various leaders begin to promote a multiplicity of per-

*sonally related causes, the will of the people to follow is
replaced by subdued antagonism. Personal incentives are
lost. Inertia, discontent and conflict develop. The ensuing
tension is a strong factor in the failure to maintain the
purpose-centeredness of many churches. (31:207)*

The experience of a Baptist Church is one that well illustrates
the effect of years of internal strife. The town, with a population
of 5000, had only one other fundamental testimony. Being on the
outskirts of a major city, the town was a growing community.
The edifice was a modern brick structure with a fine parking lot
and a beautiful adjoining parsonage. It had all the material
advantages for establishing a strong congregation. In spite of
these advantages, the congregation has seldom been able to
sustain an attendance above fifty because of serious internal
strife.

The external appearance of a church edifice can also be a
factor in the lack of growth and development. This was one of the
reasons why Faith Baptist Church, Oakville, Ontario, did not
experience growth. They met for years in an old frame building.
The small basement was damp and dreary. Back in the fifties
there were few homes near the site. During the late sixties and
the seventies beautiful $50,000 to $80,000 homes were erected.
The population grew from a few hundred people to over 20,000
and yet the congregation remained around the fifty mark. The
church was an isolated island in the midst of a growing community. Yet, within a matter of months, through relocation and
erection of a new building, the congregation experienced excellent growth.

Circumstances can arise over which the church has no control.
Langstaff Baptist Church of Thornhill, Ontario, was literally cut
off from its field of service because of the rerouting of highway 7.

A church might be located in an area that undergoes a land
use change. Faith Baptist Church, Sarnia, Ontario, faced this
when their rural community became an industrial belt for the
city. The residents moved away and left the church without a
community to minister to!

A significant population shift can also bring about a church
crisis. Several years ago a new work was started in Elliott Lake,
Ontario. When the mines faced a sharp cutback, the major part
of the population moved away. The congregation faced a 100%
exit.

A socio economic class change can bring about a church crisis.
Hundreds of churches in North American cities have faced such

an issue. This was one of the factors that led to the dissolution of Pape Avenue Baptist Church, Toronto. Most of the members were driving in from other communities with a higher economic level. The church had ceased to minister effectively to the adults of the area. Gradually, more and more members became discouraged. It did not take much leadership to get the people to sell the building and let the members go their own way.

Much more could be said about the reasons that contribute to a church crisis. The reader is encouraged to read, "Why Churches Die," by Dr. Hollis L. Green. In it he outlines thirty-five reasons why churches sicken and die.

II. Procedure to Follow a Church in Transition

To properly deal with this kind of situation, one needs to gather considerable material dealing with the congregation, the community and the edifice. You will note in the Appendix a fact sheet used by the Fellowship Baptist Home Mission Board.

Is the situation irreversible? This can be determined by seeking out answers to a number of questions:

1. Is there a core of families left to carry on a witness?
2. Are the remaining families of a mind to work together?
3. Are the families talented enough to furnish a well-rounded ministry of outreach?
4. Does the community warrant a continuing testimony?
5. Is the edifice suitable for a self-sustaining congregation?
6. Is the church site visible and accessible?
7. What about the pastoral relationship?

Gradually you will note a combination of several related things that brought about the church crisis.

What about the pastor in this situation? Should he continue to seek to salvage the church? In most cases it is best for the pastor to move on and let the congregation seek fresh leadership. It is very difficult, once a church is down, to regain strength under the present pastoral leadership. The church generally needs a new voice and different leadership in order to bring about changes that will lead to growth.

Study the community carefully. Is there another evangelical church in the area? How far away is another sister church? What is the median age of the adult population? Search out the school enrollment and the number of new housing starts. Is it an established area or is the population transient?

The edifice needs to be examined from the standpoint of ministry. Is it apt for Sunday School growth? Can it meet the needs of the functions you wish to carry on? Is it attractive and in keeping with the rest of the community? What would be the cost of renovations?

After such a study you will be in a better position to give a partial answer as to whether or not a ministry should be maintained in that area. It could well be that it would be best for the congregation to merge with another church. Another alternative is to sell the assets and start a new work in another community.

There is a Baptist Church that is over 100 years old which has been a small work for years. Due to a number of factors, the congregation has been reduced to just a few members today. The edifice is limited as to the functions that can be carried on. The location of the church is less than two kilometers from a strong sister church. The community is also less than two kilometers from a strong sister church. The community is not densely populated and thus the field is really small for the church. This is the type of situation where a church does not have sufficient reasons for continuing a ministry. It would be better for such a church either to sell and reinvest the assets in another work, or merge with the sister church taking its assets into the combined work.

After you have established the validity of maintaining a church in transition, turn to pastoral leadership. As indicated, almost without fail, there should be new pastoral guidance. If the present pastor was not successful in saving the congregation, no amount of transfusion will suffice. The church needs fresh leadership, yes, a pastor especially suited for replanting the work. It's a case of examining the church and community and seeking the face of God for the right man. And God has a man for every situation. It's a matter of seeking him out and praying him in!

The remaining members of the congregation should be prepared for new leadership. At this point the denominational head of home missions can give a church guidelines for receiving a new leader so that they will know what to expect. In this way, the congregation will be prepared for changes and a different type of ministry.

Example of a Church Replanter

Pastor John Roberts of Faith Baptist Church, Oakville, Ontario, is a model replanter. He combines gentleness with strength. He loves people and is a skillful listener. His wife is ideal for working with and helping people.

It was in June, 1975, that I met with the leaders of Faith Baptist. They traced the struggles through the years. They had meager results in a community with such great potential. They had been led recently by a fine student pastor who, due to his heavy academic schedule, was limited in his outreach.

This was the situation when Pastor Roberts began his ministry in November, 1975, after a nine year ministry at Flamboro Centre Baptist Church, near Hamilton, Ontario. A recommendation was made to put the church on a pastoral grant thus making it possible to call such an experienced and mature man. In addition the people were ready for a change, even a relocation, if the new pastor thought it necessary.

One of the first steps Pastor Roberts took was to locate a fine two acre site on the main street of North Oakville. Working with a Christian realtor, Clair MacLean, who also served on the Fellowship Baptist Home Mission Board, the church was able to purchase what is considered by many as a "million dollar site". In a remarkable way God led them to this choice location. Within a few days an attractive sign was placed on the lot, seen by thousands, daily, as they used the busy thoroughfare. This helped change the image of the church in the eyes of the community. It did something else, as well, it gave the members a tremendous sense of accomplishment and expectation.

It was not long before the Sunday School and morning services started to show a fine increase in attendance. The offerings in a sixteen month period went from $1656.00 a month to $2903.00.

Replanting calls for a different type of pulpit ministry, other than the *status quo* or regular run of sermon material. The pastor must seek to direct and challenge his people with a spiritual vision. In the case of Faith Baptist, the congregation soon took to the new emphasis and the mature leadership of their new pastor. Thus they were ready to follow his leadership concerning a physical and geographical change.

At times, selling a building that has been used for years can be an emotional strain on the part of certain members. We know that God does not dwell in buildings, but people do! While many will not hesitate to sell their residences in order to purchase a better house, these same people will object to selling their "sacred building'. You hear such expressions as "We were married there," or "My son was baptized there". These expressions of sentiment must be understood but not allowed to hold back the progress of the church.

Another argument used against selling an old building concerns the potential purchaser. Congregations have struggled over whether their building should be sold to a false-cult such as the Mormons. The excuse used is that the cult is being helped by purchasing your building. Actually, the cult is helping the church by purchasing the building, without which your new building program might be held up.

Replanting generally involves new pastoral leadership, a readiness on the part of the remnant for a changed ministry and an openness to new ideas and methods. This, plus faith and the blessing of God, can bring new life to old bones.

Chapter 20

HE THAT ENDURES

The church planter will be tempted to give up time after time. Perseverance is needed to cope with the complexities of church planting. However, "He that endures" will likely reap the happy establishment of a church that will honour Jesus Christ. But before the day of rejoicing, comes numerous trying experiences. The church planter will come to understand what it means to face opposition, frustration and disappointments. There are times when things will not turn out as planned. People will let him down. Promises will be broken. Other churches will compete for his families. He might be ostracized by fellow pastors who feel threatened by his presence. How does a church planter cope with such experiences?

I. Recognize the Providence of God

The church planter should recognize the Providence of God in his life. After all that is said and done, it is the work of God! It is His church. Moses, called of God to lead the Israelites from Egypt to the Promised Land, prayed in Psalm 90:14,15: "O satisfy us early with thy mercy; that we may rejoice and be glad all our days. Make us glad according to the days wherein thou has afflicted us, and the years wherein we have seen evil." Moses did not really have an easy time with his people but he recognized the Providence of God at work in his life and ministry. You will not be able to control all the things that are likely to befall you in the ministry, but you can control the spirit with which you meet them. Let it be the spirit of Moses who went on to pray in Psalm 90:17: "And let the beauty of the Lord our God be upon us: and establish thou the work of our hands upon us; yea the work of our hands establish thou it." This is our desire. We want our lives to manifest Jesus Christ. You note the final request of Moses when he asked God to establish the work of his hands. What better or more permanent work can be done than to establish a church that will last until our Lord returns.

II. Find Courage in the Word of God

The first church planter, the Apostle Paul, blazed a trail for all church planters. Now Paul did not have an easy time. This is how he describes some of his experiences:

Are they ministers of Christ? I am more; in labours more abundant, in stripes above measure, in prisons more frequent, in deaths oft. Of the Jews five times received I forty stripes save one. Twice was I beaten with rods, once was I stoned, twice I suffered shipwreck, a night a day I have been in the deep; in journeyings often, in perils of waters, in perils of robbers, in perils in the city, in perils in the wilderness, in perils in the sea, in perils among false brethren... beside those that are without, that which cometh upon me daily, the care of all the churches. (2 Cor. 11:23-28)

Yet Paul was confident as the Holy Spirit assured him in 1 Cor. 10:13: "God is faithful, who will not suffer you to be tempted above that ye are able". God will not forsake a pastor in the ministry of establishing a church. At the right time doors will open and things will settle into place. But we, like Paul, must do our work faithfully. Note how Paul exhorts pastors in 2 Tim. 2:1-5:

Thou therefore, my son, be strong in the grace that is in Christ Jesus. And the things that thou hast heard of me among many witnesses, the same commit thou to faithful men, who shall be able to teach others also. Thou therefore endure hardness, as a good soldier of Jesus Christ. No man that warreth entangleth himself with the affairs of this life; that he may please him who hath chosen him to be a soldier. And if a man also strive for masteries, yet is he not crowned, except he strive lawfully.

III. Recognize the Call of God

The church planter must recognize that his call is from God. Any other motivation for church planting will come to nought. There is the danger of building a name for yourself. "This is what I have done" when we labour in the flesh for our own self-image. It is possible to speak using spiritual terms and to parrot a biblical message wearing a pious mask. All self seeking is of no avail. If your call is from God, do the work in a way that will honour Him. The end does not justify the means! One Sunday, the buses of a large Baptist Church in Southern Ontario were out picking up their regular route. A few children were waiting at their corner. A new church got underway and put on a bus which went ahead of the buses from the other church and actually encouraged, and in some cases, secured a number of children. The pastor of the new church was fully aware of the situation, but he was out to build a large Sunday School. Had he not advertised that in the coming year there would be one thousand decisions? He had to have them, one way or another! Needless to say, there was much confusion and disrepute was brought to the name of Christ.

IV. Remember your Objective

The church planter must remember his objective. What has God planned for this particular community? From this point you plan your means of achieving it. In doing so you need to recall that Rome was not built in a day. It takes time to foster and cultivate a new church before it develops and matures. Growing pains are not easy to live with but they are necessary. Success that comes easily is not always worth-while.

Dr. Hal MacBain was holding services for Pastor Don Robins of the Temple Baptist Church, Lower Sackville, Nova Scotia. At the time the new congregation was meeting in a very limited building that was not at all suitable for a growing church. The auditorium was packed for all services. Commenting on the situation he said it was too bad the church was so limited with its facilities. He added that perhaps this will make a stronger church for people will better appreciate what they must work to accomplish.

V. Remember the Base upon which the Church Started

The church planter must remember the base upon which he is building. His congregation is small and untried. It is very different from a self-supporting church. In a new work the people are getting acquainted. New friendships are being formed. People are probably from various denominational backgrounds. Time is needed to orient them to your doctrinal stand and leadership.

One church planter complained about the lack of support for the Sunday evening services. After considering their backgrounds, he realized only a few were in the habit of attending two services a Sunday at their former churches. The rest were from churches which emphasized a Sunday morning service except for an occasional special evening hour for a concert. Consequently, it took a period of time to motivate the people to participate in a full range of Sunday services.

VI. Maintain a Good Relationship with your Own Family

Paul outlines the duties of pastors in I Timothy 3 and gives the following charge concerning the pastoral family: "A bishop then must be blameless, the husband of one wife, vigilant, sober, of good behaviour. . . one that ruleth well his own house, having his children in subjection with all gravity; for if a man know not how to rule his own house, how shall he take care of the Church of God." A good family relationship does much to help the pastor's personal health and vitality. There is a vital connection between a man's morale in his home and his morale in his work.

Foremost in the family is the relationship between husband and wife. Actually, if a pastor does not have the proper relationship with his wife, how can he expect to relate well with his church members? His home is a model of how a Christian couple live together to the glory of God. This is done best when the husband identifies with his wife. Gene Getz stresses this:

The husband must identify with his wife — her pain, her heartaches, her struggles, her weaknesses, her anxieties, her stresses. Remember that Christ's love caused Him to identify with us. To love your wife as Christ loved the Church means identification with her. In fact, Peter laid on Christian husbands the leaviest injunction of all — "Husbands, in the same way be considerate as you live with your wives, and treat them with respect as the weaker partner and heirs with you of the gracious gift of life, so that nothing will hinder your prayers (1 Peter 3:7)" There is no question what Peter had in mind. We must identify with their weaknesses and we must understand and minister to them. Furthermore, Peter actually stipulates that some

*men's prayers are hindered because they do not "love their
wives as Christ loved the church". (16:66)*

The church planter has a real responsibility in loving and
understanding his children. At times, due to the pressures of his
work and the pressing need to produce, he may lose patience and
blame his children for his own faults. This type of projection can
lead to an overbearing attitude where a child be disciplined too
severely. William Hulme gives the following insight:

> *In the parent's frustration over his own growth he may
> demand too much from his children. He does that which the
> Scriptural directive warns against — he overcorrects. If this
> overcorrection is pursued relentlessly it may foster either
> the broken-spirited conformist whose rebellion must be
> carried out surreptitiously or the angry rebel whose con-
> formity has to be equally as surreptitious. In other words
> parents are prompt to demand from their children what
> they cannot be themselves. When siblings engage in
> bickering, the parents are quick to silence the strife. At the
> same time father and mother can really go at each other and
> the children know it. Or if the children begin to complain
> about this or that, the parents let them know in no uncertain
> terms that such complaining must stop. Yet these same
> parents may complain about the neighbours, the relatives,
> the inlaws, the church. . . or even about each other, and the
> children have to listen. What we cannot tolerate in our
> children we have a way of justifying in ourselves. (36:96)*

Your wife and children can be of immeasurable help in church
planting. Their input can be tripled by a loving and understanding husband and father. A good home atmosphere can
help you persevere in the presence of opposition and difficulties
in your work.

This does not mean there will not be problems and at times
tension in your home. Ann Landers has well said: "Marriage is
fun, its living together that's tough". Working out family
situations is good training for working out church situations.

VII. Carefully receive New Members

The church planter should carefully receive new members.
Two dangers face the fundamental church today. The first is to
be on the guard against unsaved people uniting with the
membership. The second is to be on guard against receiving
disgruntled members from other fundamental churches.

It is possible for unsaved people to join a church. Someone has well said there are two kinds of Baptist, those who are saved and those who are not saved. A mere profession is not enough for membership. Pastors and deacons have a right to ask new believers if there has been a change in their life. "Therefore if any man be in Christ, he is a new creature: old things are passed away; behold, all things are become new. (2 Cor. 5:17) A Shantyman missionary was visiting a pastor and told about a Baptist church in New Brunswick where the unsaved members out number the born-again believers. It is sad day for the church when this happens.

It is possible for members from other churches to unite with your work because of the freshness and vitality of a new organization. It is wise to check the spirit with which they left their former church. A disgruntled, critical, negative member in one church might after a time become the same in a new church. Many church planters have been faced with a severe problem of perseverance because of taking in members who had not made things right in their former churches. A phone call to the former pastors will give you insight as to what to expect.

VIII. Maintain Personal Quiet Time with the Lord

This is of upmost necessity for your work. Jesus Christ talks about serving one master in Matthew 6:24. He goes on to talk about everyday experiences of life and shows what our priority should be: "Seek ye first the Kingdom of God and his righteousness; and all these things shall be added unto you. (Matt. 6:33)

The devil will do all he can to disrupt your devotional period with the Lord. If it is not the telephone it will be the door bell. If it is not a member of your family it will be yourself with a wandering mind. Three things will assist in making the quiet time meaningful: a definite period, a definite place and a definite procedure. We are creatures of habit. What we do today will influence what we do tomorrow. Therefore, establish a set period of time when you will be alone in meditation and prayer. A special place will enhance this period as you seek to be quiet before the Lord. A planned procedure where you start with the Word, followed by praise and prayer will assist in making the time honourable to the Lord. Godfrey Catanus who serves the Filipino Baptist Church, Toronto, has a motto: "No devotion, no breakfast".

IX. Keep on Reading

It is easy to be caught up with your work of visitation, meetings and routine studies, that little time is left for serious reading. You would be wise to carefully choose your reading material. Schedule regular reading hours. Take a speed reading course. Dixon Burns who taught Homiletics at Toronto Bible College for many years would use his summer months to read as many as 10,000 pages. Books are your bread and butter. Do not neglect them.

This is a day when you can play tapes of sermons inspired by great Bible teachers. Lectures and actual courses can be taked by way of tapes. Seminaries and Bible Colleges have tapes for rent through their libraries. Many pastors have a cassette recorder in their cars and thus make use of driving time for studies.

X. Fellowship with Others

This can be a cold world without friends. Others engaged in a fundamental ministry can help as you share and relate together. Attend Bible conferences where you can hear outstanding Bible teachers. The Muskoka Baptist Conference in Ontario under the leadership of Rev. Richard Holliday is having an expanding ministry. Annual Founders Week Conferences at Moody Bible Institute, Bethel College, St. Paul, Minnesota and Central Baptist Seminary, Toronto are serving to provide inspiration and edification to pastors. Taking time for a few days apart will be repaid with renewed energy and zeal.

Example of a Church Planter who Knew how to Persevere

"Triumph in Adversity" would be a good title for the experiences of Pastor Charles Arndt in his two church planting situations. He is a model of a church planter who has borne up under great emotional pressures. Problem after problem arose to challenge his imagination as to how to meet them. At times it would seem that he faced a cement wall with no way around or through it. It is at such a time that church planters are fully dependent on the Lord.

Charles Arndt was 34 when he moved from Faith Baptist Church, New Hamburg, Ontario, where he had just established a work, to Brockville, Ontario. So many things happened in the opening month that he might well have packed his furniture and left the city.

In a new church where people are untried you will find

disappointments. One of the young men Charles Arndt counted on was a graduate of a Bible college. Along with his wife they were looked upon as the backbone of the church. Nothing of the kind followed. Rather, the couple's immaturity became a heavy weight upon the pastor.

A church building came up for sale for $39,000.00 including an attached parsonage on a fine landscaped two acre lot. It was only a matter of time when this building became too small and the parsonage rooms were taken over for services.

During the time when the pastor lived with his family in the attached parsonage, he had no trouble closing at 12 noon. The roast in the kitchen occupied the minds of the congregation as the aroma circulated throughout the auditorium.

Sunday morning was a hectic day for Mrs. Arndt. The beds had to be made, the rooms placed in order and everything set because the Sunday School classes occupied the parsonage. You can imagine the rush with three little children to prepare and feed before the early Sunday School hour. It was an increasing burden when one of the children was sick on a Sunday. The Arndts really had no privacy to speak of.

How do you put a small child to bed at night with 60 to 70 people singing to their hearts content next door to the bedroom? Yet Sunday after Sunday Mrs. Arndt stood by her husband and worked with him, sharing in the hardships of church planting.

Still the congregation grew, from a small group of 25 to 180 within a thirty month period. God had His hand on this church planter and brought abundant fruit.

Personal problems followed when the pastor moved out of the parsonage to a newly purchased house. In many respects it was a dream house from outward appearance. A large family room served to host church families. A full basement served to provide a game room for youth.

On the day the pastor moved in, he was sitting on the davenport relaxing. Of course everything was in a turmoil and it was raining outside. As he sat there he discovered that there was a drip. He looked at his hand and sure enough there was water coming from the roof. Little did he know at that time that this was the introduction to what had to be the most leaky house in town! They learned in subsequent days that the basement leaked every time it rained. It was not unusual for the family to come home on a Sunday and to have to spend Sunday evening mopping up water in the basement or carrying it out by the bucketful and dumping it outside. This became a routine. Actually it was such a routine that he eventually painted the basement floor so that it could be called a swimming pool and thus make a joke out of it. Otherwise it would have been more than they could have borne.

As the work grew they planned a potluck supper for the monthly Sunday School Teachers and Officers meeting. So with great anticipation and, announcing it well in advance, encouraging the teachers, they worked hard to see that everything was ready. Mrs. Arndt spent considerable time in getting various things baked as far as food was concerned. They sat down waiting for the people to come. It was set for 6:30 p.m. but no one was present. By 6:45 p.m. no one came. It got to be 7, 7:30 p.m. and 8:00 p.m. and not one individual had come. They wound up having their potluck Teachers and Officers meeting all by themselves. What discouragement! They were heartbroken.

How did the Arndts respond to these and many other circumstances of trial and tribulation? They found that these experiences had drawn them closer to the Lord. They sensed their full dependence upon the Holy Spirit. They can testify that in the midst of a problem God gave them grace and patience. In one situation when the financial pressure was extremely heavy they sought the face of God in prayer and asked Him to answer. It was at such a time they received a gift from another church, over and above the grant they were receiving from the Fellowship Baptist Home Mission Board.

Pastor and Mrs. Arndt can pray the thoughts of Dr. A.W. Tozer:

> *I accept hard work and small rewards in this life. I ask for no easy place. I shall try to be blind to the little ways that could make life easier. If others seek the smoother path I shall try to take the hard way without judging them too harshly. I shall expect opposition and try to take it quietly when it comes. Or if as sometimes it falleth out to Thy servants, I should have grateful gifts pressed upon me by Thy kindly people, stand by me then and save me from the blight that often follows. Teach me to use whatever I receive in such manner that it will not injure my sould nor diminish my spiritual power. And if in Thy permissive providence honour should come to me from Thy church, let me not forget in that hour that I am unworthy of the least of Thy mercies, and that if men knew me as intimately as I know myself they would withhold their honours or bestow them' upon others more worthy to receive them.*
>
> *And now, O Lord of heaven and earth, I consecrate my remaining days to Thee; let them be many or few as Thou*

wilt. Let me stand before the great or minister to the poor and lowly; that choice is not mine, and I would not influence it if I could. I am Thy servant to do Thy will, and that will is sweeter to me than position or riches or fame and I choose it above all things on earth or in heaven. (97)

Chapter 21

Central Baptist Church,
London, Ontario

LET'S GET ON WITH THE JOB

It's one thing to know the method of church planting, but another thing to be involved in church planting. It's one thing to desire to see churches planted and another thing to invest your time, talent and treasury in church planting. Now let's get the job done. We have all the tools.

I. We Have His Presence

Can you imagine the mighty power of God at your disposal? This is what Jesus Christ promised in Matt. 28:18: "All power is given unto Me, in heaven and in earth. Go ye therefore." When we go forth in His name, we go in His strength and with His Spirit. Too often men have laboured in their own strength and power. In the ministry of church planting we must work as Spirit-filled people. This is why what you are is so important. The message must be manifested by the life. The world needs to see our faith demonstrated in bodily form. Would to God we could have a repeat of the first Christian Church that J.P. Phillips wrote about in the preface to his translation of Acts:

> *The reader is stirred because he is seeing Christianity, the real thing, in action for the first time in human history....Here we are seeing the Church valiant and unspoiled — a body of ordinary men and women joined together in an unconquerable fellowship never before seen*

on this earth... a fellowship of men and women so united in love and faith that He can work in them and through them.... Consequently it is a matter of sober historical fact that never before has any small body of ordinary people so moved the world that their enemies could say, with tears of rage in their eyes, that these men "have turned the world upside down."

II. We Have His Message

Thank God we have His message and not the message of a mere man. As Paul proclaimed: "For I delivered unto you first of all that which I also received, how that Christ died for our sins according to the scriptures; and that he was buried, and that he rose again the third day according to the scriptures." We need not apologize for the glorious gospel which we preach. The liberal church has seen how the social gospel does not work. Their pews are being vacated by the scores. The Roman Catholic Church is in a transitional period. It is difficult to determine how things are going to turn out for the Church of Rome. About ten major Roman Catholic seminaries have been closed since 1960. Whereas not one major conservative Bible college or seminary has closed in the same period. This is our day as evangelicals. The world needs to hear the message of hope which we have through Jesus Christ.

Our society has seen the gospel transform alcoholics, drug addicts and hardened criminals. We have seen in recent months several remarkable conversions in the lives of men like Charles Colson, Cleaver Eldridge and Larry Flynt, the former publisher of Hustler, a magazine that is even more offensive to biblical standards of morality than Playboy, according to an editorial in Christianity Today. Yes, we need the determination of Paul when he declared: "So, as much as in me is, I am ready to preach the gospel to you that are at Rome also. For I am not ashamed of the gospel of Christ: for it is the power of God unto salvation to every one that believeth." (Romans 1:15,16).

III. We Have His Commission

In what is commonly known as "The Great Commission" we are given the mandate to go into all the world. It is interesting to note in Acts 1:8 that we are to begin in our own "Jerusalem". This is a command to plant churches as people are reached with the gospel.

With the commission there is a vision of a lost and dying world without Christ. We need to see ourselves, as we would have been without Christ. We are thankful that Jesus Christ has saved us from our sins. We are thankful that Jesus Christ has given us new life. And now we are thankful that Jesus Christ has given us His message to proclaim.

We sense with Paul our commission: "For necessity is laid upon me; yea, woe is unto me, if I preach not the gospel (1 Cor. 9:16)!" It is time we allow God the Holy Spirit to have His way with our lips and lives. Let us be opened and clean vessels through which He may be proclaimed bringing hope to troubled hearts.

IV. We Have the Manpower

Our Bible colleges and conservative seminaries have no shortage of students preparing for Christian service. This is our greatest heritage. The 410 churches of the Fellowship Baptists in Canada serve as an example of the manpower available in a fundamental denomination. It is amazing to look at the enrollment of Fellowship Baptist youth in the following schools in January, 1978:

Central Baptist Seminary, Toronto	140 students
London Baptist Seminary, London	110 students
Northwest Baptist Theological College & Seminary, Vancouver	135 students
Ontario Bible College & Seminary, Toronto	150 (Approx.)
Seminaire Baptiste Evangelique au Canada	100 (Approx.)
Other Bible Schools — U.S. and Canada	150 (Approx.)

There is no shortage of pastors in our evangelical circles. In fact there is a surplus. The late Pope Paul VI in a recent article was alarmed at the number of priests and nuns giving up their vows and turning to secular employment. In many liberal Protestant churches there is a real shortage of pastors. However, in the Providence of God, we have the manpower to greatly expand in the field of church planting.

V. We have the Financial Resources

Never have the evangelical churches been as wealthy as they are today. There is no shortage of money in the hands of God's people. The evangelical church has tremendous financial resources at its disposal. The world renowned Peoples Church, Toronto, founded by Dr. Oswald J. Smith, and now ably led by his son, Dr. Paul B. Smith, is now raising $1,500,000 a year for missions. Across Canada there are many evangelical churches with annual budgets ranging from $200,000 to $500,000. In the United States there are many evangelical churches with annual budgets exceeding $1,000,000.

One needs only to look at the buildings now being operated by evangelicals to determine the financial resources. Large buildings are now under construction to house Christian day-care centres and senior citizen homes. Christian camps are increasing throughout North America.

Another indication of financial backing is seen in the development of Christian TV programming. Several of these regular presentations rank with some of the finest productions of the stations. And they pay for themselves. The Peoples Church, Toronto, decided to televise their Sunday morning services. The financial response has covered the total cost. Yes, we have the financial resources to get the job done, to the glory of God, if we can motivate our people to a high level of stewardship.

VI. We have seen the Results of New Churches

New churches provide resources for missions. In a real way new churches serve as a key to missionary outreach. In 1972, First Baptist Church, Cochrane, Ontario, was re-opened after being closed for several years. Receiving home mission assistance, the church, two years later, was able to send offerings for missionary outreach. It is not uncommon to receive from new churches, cheques ranging from $500.00 to $2,000.00.

New churches provide personnel for mission fields. Dr. Hal MacBain needed a farmer to help set up the bee industry in Colombia, South America. It is noteworthy that John De Zeew, a farmer from a home mission church in Brockville, Ontario, came forward and filled the post. A school teacher was needed for missionary children in Colombia. Again God stirred the heart of a member of a home mission church, as Miss Beverley Laidlaw of the new Forest Hills Baptist, Dartmouth, Nova Scotia, responded to the call.

New churches are being used of the Lord to reach the unsaved. It was a stirring night at the Annual Convention of the Fellowship of Evangelical Baptist Churches in Canada, meeting at Niagara Falls, Ontario, for the Rally of Witness. The auditorium was packed to capacity for the Home Mission presentation. One of the moving experiences was the testimony of the 1973 Miss Prince Edward Island, Miss Amy Vessey. This young lady during her reigning year started attending the services of the new Grace Baptist Church, Charlottetown. This is her testimony:

I came to know Christ as my personal Saviour, August 11, 1974. Since that time I was baptized and joined Grace Baptist Church. I thank God for the testimony of this Bible-believing church. It was through relatives and friends that had gone to this church that I came to know about it. I just thank God for the opportunity that I have now to work through the visitation program in our church in which I am really involved to reach other people because if someone hadn't told me about it I wouldn't be saved right now. I just want to tell others of the great thing God has done for me.

Was it worthwhile to invest several hundred dollars a month to get this church started? For all eternity, Amy and others are going to rejoice because people cared for their souls.

VII. Now is the Time for New Churches

If ever the world needs new churches this is the hour! The time has come to rise up and plant churches across our continent. No one can question our authority for it is biblical. None can question the method for it was used by the apostles. No one can question the results for it is God's way. No one can question its effectiveness for it reaches every strata of society. It makes no difference, you will find churches in the slums and in the affluent communities.

"Let's get on with the job" is the burden of Rev. Roy Lawson, the new General Secretary of The Fellowship of Evangelical Baptist Churches in Canada. Entering this post, October 1, 1977, Roy Lawson brings into his office, a dedicated mind, an energetic body and over twenty years of full and fruitful ministry.

Born in the home of a pastor, the ministry is all he has ever known. Preaching comes natural to him. A graduate of the London Bible Institute, he commenced his ministry as the first full time pastor of the Broadway Baptist Church, Tillsonburg, Ontario, in 1962. This was a branch work of Otterville Baptist, Otterville, Ontario. Total offerings were $39.00 a week and so the church wanted him to work part time. Roy Lawson asked them: "Are you willing to take a step of faith?" They responded and he did not take a part time job. Within a year the church offerings had increased to $300.00 a week! The services had grown far beyond the capacity of the building.

Looking back on the way God used him, Roy Lawson attributes visitation as the key to the achieved growth. He asked people to give him names. He would personally visit these folks and show a genuine interest in their spiritual needs. As a result, hearts were moved by the Holy Spirit as the Word was sown.

A second factor was the great stress laid on youth. The church would rent the Tillsonburg Arena. Here throngs of youth would gather for ice skating. Roy Lawson would lead the devotional period and here he would get down to the nuts and bolts of the Christian faith. The young people soon sensed that this pastor cared for them.

The pulpit ministry was a third factor. He really worked on this. He preached the gospel and drew in the net, again and again. He believed in giving an invitation and urged people to respond to the claims of God. He emphasized strong doctrinal messages. He was concerned that people not only knew Jesus Christ as Saviour, but understood their Christian faith and could stand up against false doctrines and cults.

The Tillsonburg ministry was followed by a similar experience at Bethel Baptist Church, Strathroy, Ontario. An added feature was the planting of a daughter church, Faith Evangelical Baptist at Watford, Ontario. He did not think that Bethel Baptist was too small to begin a daughter church, nor too weak to branch out. Rather he found that a concentrated outreach actually strengthens the mother church. He trusted God the Holy Spirit to give gifts and to raise up spiritual leadership from within the new daughter church.

This young preacher was called at the age of 35 to the pulpit of Central Baptist Church, London, Ontario, which is one of the largest and most influential pulpits in fundamental ministries in Canada. Here under his ministry the church prospered and grew. Missions were expanded. Sunday School attendance records were set.

He was next called to be the first national youth leader of the Fellowship Baptist Young People's Association. Travelling from East to West he stirred thousands of youth to a higher spiritual commitment to the Lord Jesus Christ. Scores of churches were moved by the Holy Spirit through the ministry of the Word. Under his leadership, Summer Workers in Fellowship Thrust (SWIFT) came into existence. This ministry has seen several hundred young people give their summers to the gospel ministry throughout Canada and in several foreign lands.

Entering the top post of the Fellowship Baptists, he has envisioned a great forward moving thrust to the glory of God. This is best seen by the accomplishments of his first year of leadership.

His initial step was to handle Project '78 which featured a special missionary endeavour for the French Canada Board. Never in the history of Fellowship Baptists has there been such a response. At the Rally of Witness in Vancouver, British Columbia, on Wednesday, October 26, 1977, over $74,000.00 was reported in offerings and pledges. Previous high was the Project '76 sponsored by the Fellowship Foreign Board which amounted to $11,000.00.

A second enterprise was the erection of a two story addition to the home office in Willowdale, Ontario. Here much needed space has been added to care for the growing staff and to handle the developing ministry.

Next he assembled a group of leaders to plan with him for contemplated growth and expansion. He senses the need of a team spirit. He is not afraid to delegate. He believes the work can best be done as he motivates and provides leadership.

Thank God in all of this Roy Lawson has emphasized the spiritual. He knows it is "Not by might, nor by power" but by the Spirit of God working through dedicated vessels. He would agree with the statement of Norman B. Jerome who told about an executive of a missionary society operating in a foreign land: "Our candidates are screened and groomed, educated and analyzed. They are sent to orientation schools and given special courses in linguistics and cultural anthropology, yet we fail. Why? W. Graham Scroggie put his finger on the trouble. 'We have banked more on prestige than prayer. We have organized more than we have agonized. We have allowed ritual to obscure reality. We have thought more of conferences than of consecration. In short, we have displaced the Holy Spirit and it is high time that we recognized the cause of our spiritual stringency.'" (101:11)

It is high time we realize that God wants to pour out His Spirit upon and through His people today. God is waiting for a denomination — for a local church — yea, for an individual — through which He can build His Church.... "and the gates of hell shall not prevail against it." (Matt. 16:18)

CHURCH CHARTER

CALVARY BAPTIST CHURCH — MAINTOWN, NORTH AMERICA

We, the undersigned do hereby co enant together to organize the Calvary Baptist Church in Maintown, North America, and to affiliate with the Fellowship of Evangelical Baptist Churches in Canada.

We have each received the Lord Jesus Christ as our Saviour and sincerely desire to serve Him as our Lord. We have also been baptized by immersion as a testimony of our faith in Jesus Christ. We have read the attached Statement of Faith and are in agreement with it. We have also read the Church Covenant and will endeavor by God's help to lead a Christian life consistent with the principles contained therein. We have read the attached Constitution and are willing to abide by the policies set forth in this document.

1. _____
2. _____
3. _____
4. _____
5. _____
6. _____
7. _____
8. _____

PLANS AND OBJECTIVES

Appendix 1

19____

Church_____ of ....
State as far as possible your objectives for the coming year in the
following areas and how you plan to implement and reach them.

Attendance goals
  Sunday School

  Morning Service

  Evening Service

Offering Goals

Organizations — Include plans for starting specific
organizations or plans for improving present organizations.

Other Plans

_____
Church Planter

LETTER TO
A NEWBORN BABY

Dear Susan:

I am happy to welcome you as our very newest member to the Sunday School of Dovercourt Road Baptist Church. Your parents have been expecting your arrival and so have we at Dovercourt Church.

God has afforded you the high privilege of being born into a Christian home. Your parents love Jesus Christ. They like to read His Word in your home. They will seek to use the Word of God in raising you. Their deep desire is that someday you will ask Jesus Christ to be your Lord and Saviour.

Your parents know how well we care for our babies at Dovercourt Church. The nursery is carefully supervised by Mrs. Wilbur Long. Mrs. Gladys McNaught has charge of the weekly laundry of clothes and toys. And, of course, your bottle and personal belongings have their own compartment in the built-in cribs. Tell Mother not bring diapers as we provide them.

It is my prayer you will grow, as Jesus did: "In wisdom and stature, and in favour with God and man."

Your pastor,

A.T.Starr

FIELD SURVEY FORM

The Community
Name_____

Population ....

Make a geographical sketch of the community and mark it off on a map, attaching it to the Grant application. Indicate the location of other evangelical churches.

The people belong to the: High Income Group_____ Middle_____ Low _____

Approximately what percentage of the people own homes?_____

The Congregation
Membership: Men_____ Women_____ Youth under 16__
Average Attendance: _____

Sunday Services_____
Organizations (Womens, Youth, Children, etc.)

_____

_____

Brief history of the church:
Who was the founder? _____

Why was this work started? _____
What is the main problem for the work decreasing? _____
_____

Is   the   real   issue...   moral_____   financial_____
domineering individual member(s)_____ or_____?
What has the pastor done about the problem?_____
_____

What have the deacons done about the problem? _____
_____

What has the congregation done about the problem? _____
_____

Have there been any spiritual healings? Matt. 5:23,24; 18:15-17.

The Church Building and Land
Indebtedness_____ Size of property_____ Building:
Size_____ _____
Condition_____ Parking spaces_____ Location:
Good____Fair____ Poor____

Conclusion:
Give other matters of interest about the community,
congregation, church building. Write out your suggestions for
work in the community.

BIBLIOGRAPHY BOOKS

1. Anderson, Andy, *Where the Action Is.* Nashville, Tennessee: Broadman Press, 1976. 158 pp.
2. Anderson, Stanley Edwin, *Your Baptism Is Important.* London: Marshall, Morgan and Scott, 1960.
3. Anderson, T. Lee, *Church Property Building Guidebook.* Nashville, Tennessee: Convention Press, 1973. 188 pp.
4. Baumann, Dan, *All Originality Makes a Dull Church.* Santa Ana, California: Vision House Publishers, 1976 141 pp.
5. Belew, M. Wendell, *Churches and How They Grow.* Nashville, Tennessee: Broadman Press, 1971. 144 pp.
6. Benjamin, Paul, *The Growing Congregation.* Lincoln, Illinois: Lincoln Christian College Press, 1972. 95 pp.
7. Bennett, Jr. F. Russell, *The Fellowship of Kindred Minds.* Atlanta, Georgia: Home Mission Board, 1974. 160 pp.
8. Bettger, Frank, *How I Raised Myself from Failure to Success in Selling.* New York: Prentice-Hall, 1953 276.
9. Blackwood, Andrew, *Pastoral Work.* Grand Rapids: Baker Book House, 1971.
10. Carleton, W.A., *The Growth of the Early Church.* Nashville, Tennessee: Convention Press, 1970. 212 pp.
11. Clark, Carl A., *Rural Churches in Transition.* Nashville: Broadman Press, 1959. 145 pp.

12. Crowder, Rowland E., *Designing Church Buildings for Southern Baptist* Churches. Nashville: Convention Press, 1976. 65 pp.
13. Cook, Harold R., *Historical Patterns of Church Growth.* Chicago: Moody Press, 1971.
14. Currin, James H., *Starting New Missions and Churches.* Nashville: The Sunday School Board, 1971 44 pp
15. Dollar, Truman, *How to Carry Out God's Stewardship Plan.* Nashville: Thomas Nelson Inc. 1974 191 pp
16. Driggers, B. Carlisle, *Crisis or Opportunity?* Atlanta: Home Mission Board, 1977. 78 pp.
17. Dale, Robert, *Growing a Loving Church.* Nashville: Convention Press, 1974. 127 pp.
18. Falwell, Jerry, *Capturinga Town for Christ.* Old Tappan, New Jersey: Fleming H. Revell Co., 1973. 191 pp.
20. Fickett, Jr. Harold L., *Hope for Your Church.* Glendale, California: Regal Books, 1972. 159 pp.
21. Flynn, Leslie B., *How to Save Time in the Ministry.* Nashville: Broadman Press, 1966. 95 pp.
22. Foshee, Howard B., *The Ministry of the Deacon.* Nashville: Broadman Press, 1966. 125 pp.
23. Funk, Abe., *Visitation Evangelism.* Chicago: Harvest Publications, 1964.
24. Gangel, Kenneth O., *Competent to Lead.* Chicago: Moody Press, 1974. 144 pp.
25. Gerber, Vergil, *God's Way to Keep a Church Going and Growing.* Glendale, California: Regal Books, 1973. 95 pp.
26. Getz, Gene A., *The Measure of a Family.* Glendale, California: Regal Books, 1976. 166 pp.
27. Getz, Gene A., *The Measure of a Church.* Glendale, California: Regal Books, 1975. 159 pp.
28. Getz, Gene A., *Sharpening the Focus of the Church.* Chicago: Moody Press, 1974. 320 pp.
29. Glasser, Arthur, *God's Men.* Chicago: InterVarsity Press, 1968. 151 pp.
30. Graves, Allen W., *A Church at Work.* Nashville: Broadman Press, 1972. 136 pp.
31. Green, Hollis L.,*Why Churches Die.* Minneapolis, Minnesota: Bethany Fellowship, 1972. 219 pp.
32. Harrell, W.A., *Planning Better Church Buildings.* Nashville: Convention Press, 1957. 132 pp.
33. Havlik, John F., *The Evangelistic Church.* Nashville: Convention Press, 1976. 119 pp.

34. Hilgard, Ernest R., Atkinson, Richard C., Atkinson, Rita L., *Introduction to Psychology.* New York: Harcourt Brace Jovanovich, Inc. 1971. 640 pp.
35. Hodges, Melvin L., *A Guide to Church Planting.* Chicago: Moody Press, 1973. 94 pp.
36. Hulme, William *The Pastoral Care of Families.* New York: Abingdon Press, 1962. 209 pp.
37. Hyles, Jack, *The Hyles Sunday School Manual.* Murfreesboro, Tennessee: Sword of the Lord Publishers, 1969. 252 pp.
38. Hyles, Jack, *The Hyles Church Manual.* Murfreesboro, Tennessee: Sword of the Lord Publishers, 1976. 328 pp.
39. Jones, Ezra Earl, *Strategies for New Churches.* New York: Harper and Row, 1976. 178 pp.
40. Kelley, Dean M., *Why Conservative Churches are Growing.* New York: Harper and Row, 1972. 184 pp.
41. Kilgore, Robert H., *How Much a Debtor.* Atlanta: Home Mission Board.
42. Lancaster, Paul, *Here Comes Tomorrow.* Princeton, New Jersey: Dow Jones Books, 1966. 196 pp.
43. Lindsell Harold, *The Battle for the Bible.* Grand Rapids: Zondervan Publishing House, 1976. 218 pp.
44. Longenecker, Harold L., *Building Town and Country Churches.* Chicago: Moody Press, 1973. 122 pp.
45. Johnson, Gordon G. *My Church.* Chicago: Harvest Publications, 1963. 149 pp.
46. Mackenzie, R. Alex., *The Time Trap.* New York: Amacon, 1972. 192 pp.
47. Mavis, W. Curry, *Advancing the Smaller Church.* Grand Rapids: Baker Book House, 1957. 176 pp.
48. MacNair, Donald A., and Arn, Winfield C., *Ten Steps for Church Growth.* New York: Harper and Row, Publishers, 1977. 140 pp.
49. MacNair, Donald J., *The Growing Local Church.* Grand Rapids: Baker Book House, 1975. 200 pp.
50. McGavran, Donald A., and Arn, Winfield C., *Ten Steps for Church Growth.* New York: Harper and Row, Publishers, 1977. 140 pp.
51. _____,
How to Grow a Church. Glendale, California: Regal Books, 1973. 180 pp.
52. McGavran, Donald A., *How Churches Grow.* New York: Friendship Press, 1966. 189 pp.

53. McNutt, William Roy, *Polity and Practice in Baptist Churches.* The Judson Press, 1935. 274 pp.
54. Mosley, Ernest E. *Called to Joy.* Nashville: Convention Press, 1973. 156 pp.
55. Murray, Andrew, *The Lord's Table.* Chicago: Moody Press, 121 pp.
56. Neighbour, Ralph, *The Seven Last Words of the Church.* Grand Rapids: Zondervan Publishing House, 1973. 182 pp.
57. Palmer, Bernard, *Pattern for a Total Church.* Wheaton, Illinois: Victor Books, 1973. 135 pp.
58. Perkins Ernie, *Guidelines for the Pioneer Pastor.* Fairborn, Ohio: Encounter Publishing Company, 1971. 25 pp.
59. Pinson, William M. Jr., *The Local Church in Ministry.* Nashville: Broadman Press, 1973. 145 pp.
60. Powell, William, *The Urban Church Survey Manual.* Orlando, Florida: Daniels Publishers, 1972. 165 pp.
61. Privette, Jerry A., *Auditorium Planning Guide for Southern Baptist Churches.* Nashville: Broadman Press, 1975. 58 pp.
62. Rust, E. Warren, *Planbook for the Local Church in Urban Ministry.* Atlanta: Home Mission Board, 1976. 31 pp.
63. Schaeffer, Francis A., *True Spirituality.* Wheaton, Illinois: Tyndale House Publishers, 1972. 182 pp.
64. Schaller, Lyle E. and Tidwell, Charles A., *Creative Church Administration.* Nashville: Abingdon Press, 1975. 208 pp.
65. Schaller, Lyle E., *Hey, That's Our Church.* Nashville: Abingdon, 1975. 192 pp.
66. _____, *Impact of the Future.* Nashville: Abingdon, 1969. 256 pp.
67. _____, *Survival Tactics in the Parish.* Nashville: Abingdon, 1977. 208 pp.
68. Schuller, Robert H., *Your Church Has Real Possibilities!* Glendale, California: Regal Books, 1976. 186 pp.
69. Shook, Alex, *Share.* Little Britain, Ontario: Fellowship Printers, 1976.
70. Skelton, Eugene, *Ten Fastest-Growing Southern Baptist Sunday Schools.* Nashville: Broadman Press, 1974. 158 pp.
71. Smith, Ron, *The ABC of Visitation.* Kent, England: Send the Light Press, 1977.
72. Tippett, Alan R., *Church Growth and the Word of God.* Grand Rapids: Eerdmans Publishing Co., 1970. 82 pp.
73. Towns, Elmer L., *Getting a Church Started,* Impact Books, 1975. 180 pp.

74. _____, *Is the Day of the Denomination Dead?* Nashville: Thomas Nelson, 1973. 160 pp.

75. _____, *The Ten Largest Sunday Schools.* Grand Rapids: Baker Book House, 1969. 164 pp.

76. Wagner, C. Peter, *Your Church Can Grow.* Glendale: Regal Books, 1976. 176 pp.

77. Warns, Johannes, *Baptism.* Grand Rapids: Kregel Publications, 1958. 342 pp.

78. Werning, Waldo J., *Vision and Strategy for Church Growth.* Chicago: Moody Press, 1977. 124 pp.

79. Yamamori, Tetsunao, *Introducing Church Growth.* Cincinnati, Ohio: New Life Books. 1975. 256 pp.

80. Mangan, James T., *The Knack of Selling Yourself.* New York: Dartnell, 1968. 217 pp.

81. Powell, John, *Why Am I Afraid to Tell You Who I Am?* Chicago: Argus Communications, 1969

82. Walters, Barbara, *How To Talk With Practically Anybody About Practically Anything.* New York: Dell Books, 1970. 240 pp.

83. Zunin, Leonard, *Contact.* New York: Ballantine Books, 1972. 271 pp.

84. Benson, Donald, *How to Start a Daughter Church.* Quezon City, Philippines: Filkoba Press, 1972. 73 pp.

PERIODICAL ARTICLES

85. Farina, Samuel, "What's the Future of Church Publicity?" *Church Administration,* January, 1973.
86. Fletcher, George, "Before Planning a Church Building," *Church Administration,* March, 1978.
87. Hill, Leon S., "You Can Be a Better Planner," Church Administration, October, 1977.
88. Howard, Don, "Visitation," *The Evangelical Baptist,* September, 1975.
89. Matthews, C. DeWitt, "Staff Workers," *Church Administration,* january, 1973.
90. Robins, Don, "Temple Baptist," *The Evangelical Baptist,* March, 1977
91. Scott, Jack, "Preaching," *The Evangelical Baptist,* February, 1975.
92. Sheffield, "Does Your Church Need a New Constitution?" *Church Administration,* February, 1977.
93. Shields, T.T., "The Church of God," *The Gospel Witness,* Vol. 55, No. 23, February 3, 1977.
94. Touchton, Judy, "The Bi-vocational Pastor," *Home Missions,* October, 1977.
95. Weidman, Mavis L., "Your Church Building Will Determine Your Program," *The Alliance Witness,* July 12, 1961.

UNPUBLISHED MATERIALS

96. Daley, Robert, Briefing Session on Fund Raising," a paper put out by the Baptist General Conference, Chicago, Illinois.
97. Gibbs, Ralph, "Goal Setting," A paper prepared for Omark Industries, Moorestown, New Jersey.
98. Jones, Medfors H. "Motivation for Starting New Testament Churches."
99. Mitchell, J. Patrick, "How a Competent Architect Can Assist You," a paper put out by the Baptist General Conference, Chicago, Illinois.
100. Nygaard, N. "Proven Methods for Publicizing Your Church."
101. Phillips, Gordon, "The Home Mission Pastor as a Preacher," a paper given to the church planters at a conference in British Columbia.
102. Rawson, James, "Church Financing," a paper prepared for church planters at the Annual Convention of the Fellowship of Evangelical Baptist Churches in Canada, in Winnipeg, Manitoba, October, 1975.
103. Taylor, Pendley H. "Planting and Growing Churches in the Last Quarter of the 20th Century," a writing put out by the Baptist General Convention of Texas.
104. Tozer, A. W. "The Prayer of a Minor Prophet,"

105. Waltney, G. "Behold a New Thing," an article on church planting.
106. Watermann, L.P., "New Church Manual," by the Conservative Baptist Home Mission Society, Wheaton, Illinois.
106. Jerome, Norman, "Recruiting the Best for Home Missions," a paper put out by the American Sunday School Union, Philadelphia, Pennsylvania.